C000265477

THE
LONDON
TREASURY

THE
LONDON
TREASURY

A collection of cultural and historical
insights into a great city

LUCINDA HAWKSLEY

ANDRE
DEUTSCH

For Debra Mayfield, with heartfelt gratitude

THIS IS AN ANDRE DEUTSCH BOOK

Published in 2015 by André Deutsch Limited
a division of the Carlton Publishing Group
20 Mortimer Street
London W1T 3JW

10 9 8 7 6 5 4 3 2 1

Text copyright © Lucinda Hawksley, 2015
Design © André Deutsch Limited, 2015

A catalogue record for this book is available from the British Library.

ISBN 978 0 233 00482 2

Printed in Dubai

CONTENTS

1

A SHORT HISTORY
OF LONDON

In 54 BC, the Roman emperor Julius Caesar set foot briefly in Britain; near present-day London, his soldiers are said to have had a battle with a native tribe living north of the river, which ended in a truce. Roman troops came to Britain again in AD 43, this time as conquerors, under the Emperor Claudius. They arrived by boat and sailed up the River Thames to the place they would call Londinium. It became one of their most important, strategic trading ports. By AD 50 Londinium was home to over 40,000 people – until it was razed to the ground in AD 60 by Queen Boudicca of the Iceni, a rebellious native British tribe. The city was built up again, and by AD 100 had superseded Colchester as Britain's largest city and provincial capital. A small part of the original Roman-built wall around the city, now known as London Wall, can still be seen.

> *Very tall in stature, most terrifying in appearance, most fierce*
> *in the glance of her eye, with a harsh voice and a great mass*
> *of red hair that fell to her hips.*
>
> **Roman historian Dio Cassius (AD 155–235) on Boudicca**

Four centuries later, the Roman occupiers left Britain, after Emperor Constantine III withdrew his troops to fight in France. The Roman city was mostly abandoned and became a series of farming settlements. Eventually the Anglo-Saxons invaded, seized the land and created a new town, known as Lundenwic, just to the west of the old Roman walls; they also built a cathedral dedicated to St Paul inside the old city. In the mid-ninth century, Lundenwic was largely destroyed by Viking attacks. King Alfred, the West Saxon king, made peace with the Danish Vikings and began to bring the city – now called Lundenburg – back to life, still within the boundaries that the Romans had created. London was once again a thriving trading port.

LONDON FACTS

Half a century after Boudicca's attack on Londinium, the Roman historian Tacitus (AD 56–117) wrote that Boudicca's Iceni tribe and their allies, the Trinovantes, "hastened to murder, hang, burn and crucify … up to 70,000 citizens and loyal Romanized Britons".

In 1016, the Danish leader Cnut was recognized as King of England. After the death of Cnut and his sons, the English king known as Edward the Confessor came to the throne. It was he who built a royal palace and a large church (or minster) west of the city of London; the city that later grew up there thus became known as Westminster. When Edward died in 1066, a battle began for possession of the throne, ending with the victory of William the Conqueror, a Norman. London was also a fervently Christian community, with monasteries and churches in abundance. When St Paul's Cathedral burnt down in 1087, it was quickly rebuilt. In his twelfth-century history of London, cleric William Fitzstephen wrote, "London is blest in its reverence for the Christian faith, the honour of its citizens and the chastity of its women."

For centuries, London remained centred around the historic "Square Mile", better known today as the City of London. Under Henry VIII (reigned 1509–47), with the dissolution of the monasteries, much of the land that had been owned by the Church – around two-thirds of London – became the property of the King or his favourites. It began to be opened to development and London started to grow. During the reign of Elizabeth I (1558–1603) it was the largest city in Western Europe, and throughout the seventeenth century extended increasingly. London's theatreland grew dramatically too during Elizabeth I's reign: theatre was not only a great source of entertainment but also an excellent way to communicate information to a population that was largely illiterate. Her reign was known as a "Golden Age" for England, elevating London's status around the world. When King James VI of Scotland gained the English throne upon the death of Elizabeth, he became James I of England; in 1707 the two countries would be united. London, however, was not particularly keen on its new king, and the French ambassador to London was equally unimpressed, writing, "Where he wishes to assume the language of a king, his tone is that of a tyrant, and when he condescends, he is vulgar." The Golden Age was seen to have died. The city became fraught with tensions, which came to a head in 1605 with the Gunpowder Plot, an attempt to blow up the Houses of Parliament, with the King inside them.

The English Civil War (1642–51) ripped London apart, with battles pitched between Royalists and Cromwellians all over the city and its outskirts. William Lithgow, a Scot who travelled to London in 1643, wrote of barricades and fortifications all over the city, and businesses destroyed or abandoned so that "trades and trading begin to decay". London had expanded rapidly in recent decades and the population by the outbreak of the war was around 400,000, over four times greater than a century earlier. Under the Puritans, London was suppressed and Londoners terrified. Oliver Cromwell's armies closed down theatres, taverns and almost every form of entertainment. The vibrant city of Shakespeare and Queen Elizabeth I was barely recognizable. The Restoration of the monarchy and the arrival of Charles II in May 1660 was a source of great excitement and rejoicing. Samuel Pepys recorded in his diary on 31 May, "This day the month ends, I in very good health, and all the world in a merry mood because of the King's coming." Charles II's reign (1660–85) was also the time of the Great Plague, which slaughtered around 100,000 Londoners – 15 percent of the population – in the space of seven months. In just one week in September 1665, there were 7,165 recorded deaths in London. Although the plague spread throughout the country, it was believed to have been taken there by Londoners fleeing the city, where it was at its worst. The rest of the world wanted to contain it: Scotland closed its border with England and cities around the country and overseas announced a ban on trade with London. The plague is believed to have been brought to an end by another disaster, the Great Fire of London, in September 1666. Throughout it all, Charles II remained popular, but his successor, James II, was not. His turbulent reign (1685–88) was replaced by the more peaceful era of King William and Queen Mary (1688–1702).

London continued to expand into the surrounding countryside. William and Mary brought a small village outside the city into prominence when they bought a mansion in Kensington; inevitably, people wishing to associate themselves with the monarchy and aristocracy also bought land there, and gradually the area developed. Through the eighteenth century, as William and Mary, and then Queen Anne, were succeeded by the Hanoverian kings and the start of the Georgian era, London was beautified and extended even further, becoming the largest city in all Europe. It was perceived as a decadent but brilliant place, filled with entertainments, spectacles and excitement, the home of great advances in science and the arts – as well as a place rife with crime, poverty, cruelty and debauchery. Daniel Defoe (1660–1731) wrote that London was "a great and monstrous Thing".

By the time of Queen Victoria (reigned 1837–1901), London was the largest city in the world, a position it held until well into the twentieth century. It was the centre of the vast British Empire, and people travelled to and fro with ease by boat from London all over the world. Its docks grew exponentially, lined with warehouses stacked with goods from every corner of the Empire. The Industrial Revolution of c.1750–1850 had also ushered in a major societal change: the growth of the middle classes. Suddenly there was a boom in housing demand for the many large middle-class families. Victorian London was a centre of the arts, industry, shipping, engineering, manufacturing, commerce and finances, yet up until the late nineteenth century, many areas now considered central London (zones 1 and 2 on the London Underground map) were still villages outside the city. The revolution in transport that grew out of the Industrial Revolution changed the shape and size of London dramatically. As Tube lines stretched out into the countryside by the end of the nineteenth century, suburbs were created and more opportunities arose for people to move out of the overcrowded, polluted city and set up home in the more rural, cheaper places which had become easy to commute to and from.

At the end of the nineteenth century, the population of London was just under 6 million, but as the twentieth century progressed it expanded more rapidly than anyone could have imagined. Official records of 1921 show that there were approximately 7,387,000 Londoners. The population reached a peak in the 1930s; on the eve of World War II, London was home to 8,615,000. Six years later, that number had more than halved. In the ensuing decades, London's population has fluctuated widely, reaching another peak in the 1960s and a slump in the 1980s. Today, it is back to what it was in 1939 and the area known as Greater London stretches over more than 1,500 sq km (600 sq miles).

LONDON FACTS

There are many Roman roads still in existence in greater London, including Oxford Street, Kennington Road, Brixton Road, Edgware Road and Kingsland Road.

THE CITY OR THE CITY

The City of London, spelt with a capital C, always refers to the "Square Mile", the original settlement of Londinium and now the financial district at the heart of London. It has its own flag and its own coat of arms. Its motto is *Domine dirige nos*, which translates as "Lord, direct us". Around 11,000 people inhabit the City of London. The city, with a small c, refers to London as a whole. The geographic area known as Greater London is composed of 32 boroughs plus the City of London.

In the seventeenth century the City was the merchant's residence.... The whole character of the City has, since that time, undergone a complete change. At present the bankers, the merchants, and the chief shopkeepers repair thither on six mornings of every week for the transaction of business but they reside in other quarters of the metropolis, or at suburban country seats surrounded by shrubberies and flower gardens. This revolution in private habits has produced a political revolution of no small importance. The City is no longer regarded by the wealthiest traders with that attachment which everyman naturally feels for his home.... Lombard Street and Threadneedle Street are merely places where men toil and accumulate. They go elsewhere to enjoy and to expend.

Thomas Babington Macaulay, *The History of England,* **1848**

THE CITIES OF LONDON AND WESTMINSTER

When William the Conqueror arrived in Britain in the eleventh century, the ancient walls around the City of London remained intact and he agreed not to destroy the City – as long as it recognized him as king of England. Within a short time the nearby new city of Westminster grew up as the seat of power. For centuries, these two cities, Westminster and London, co-existed side by side: the City of London primarily interested in trade and commerce, the city of Westminster concerned with governing the rest of London and the country.

> *The City, St Paul's, with the river and a multitude of little boats, made a most beautiful sight as we crossed Westminster Bridge. The houses were not overhung by their cloud of smoke and they were spread out endlessly, yet the sun shone so brightly with such a pure light that was even something like the purity of one of nature's own spectacles.*
>
> **Letter written by Dorothy Wordsworth, 31 July 1802**

MAYOR OF LONDON OR LORD MAYOR OF LONDON

The City and London have separate city halls and each elects its own mayor. The Lord Mayor of London – whose full title is The Right Honourable, the Lord Mayor of London – is responsible solely for the square mile of the City of London. The Mayor of London is responsible for the entirety of Greater London. The Lord Mayor is based in the Guildhall in the City of London and lives in the Mansion House. The Mayor of London is based at City Hall, near Tower Bridge, on the south side of the river.

LONDON FACTS

The name London comes from the Roman Londinium, which in turn was derived from the area's Celtic name, Londinios, "the place of the bold one".

2

ENTERTAINMENT

EALING STUDIOS

In the 1940s and 1950s, the name Ealing was synonymous with cinema. Set up in 1904, these remain the world's oldest working film studios (now owned by the BBC). They were founded by cinema pioneer William George Barker, who bought a house called West Lodge and five acres of land, and established Barker Motion Photography Ltd. Classic Ealing comedies include:

- *Hue and Cry* (1947)
- *A Run for Your Money* (1949)
- *Whisky Galore!* (1949)
- *Passport to Pimlico* (1949)
- *Kind Hearts and Coronets* (1949)
- *The Lavender Hill Mob* (1951)
- *The Titfield Thunderbolt* (1953)
- *The Love Lottery* (1954)
- *The Ladykillers* (1955)

EGYPTIAN HALL

Opened in 1812 on Piccadilly and demolished in 1905, this was one of the most popular Georgian and Victorian theatres and exhibition centres. An early exhibition was of Napoleonic curiosities, brought back from the recent Napoleonic Wars. The building took its name from its Egyptian-influenced architecture, by G.F. Robinson. It was often described as a museum of "natural history", but its exhibits included works of art, dioramas and magic-lantern shows, as well as human performers including snake charmers and ventriloquists and the circus impresario T.P. Barnum. It was also famous for "freaks", including an emaciated man billed as "the human skeleton", a dwarf known by his stage name of Tom Thumb, and teenaged "Siamese twins". By the latter half of the Victorian era, the Egyptian Hall was attracting a more serious clientele, with explorers and adventurers holding exhibitions and lectures there.

THEATRES

- The earliest theatres in London are believed to have been introduced by the Romans, in the form of odeums or odeons, and amphitheatres open to the elements.
- During the reign of Elizabeth I, the age of theatre blossomed, with audiences swarming to see performances by William Shakespeare, Richard Burbage and other greats of the Tudor stage.
- Theatre popularity continued until the Civil War, when the Puritan leader Oliver Cromwell ordered theatres to be closed; many were destroyed.
- Following the Restoration of the monarchy in 1660, theatres reopened. The best-remembered actor from that time is Nell Gwynn, who was a seller of oranges on the streets of London until her looks launched her career as an actress. She became more famous as one of the many mistresses of Charles II; the couple had two sons.
- In 1737 a new Licensing Act was passed, controlled by the Lord Chamberlain. He was permitted to visit any theatre and declare any play unfit to be seen, with special emphasis on "obscenity". This brought new censorship to the theatre and made playwrights increasingly nervous about the risk of their plays being closed down. Anything that involved music was not classed as a play, so not included under the Act – thus a new style of theatre was spawned. Out of it would later grow the variety show, music hall and burlesque.
- The first safety curtain – made of iron – was installed at the Drury Lane Theatre in 1794.
- One of the most influential theatre designers was Frank Matcham (1854–1920), who made his name throughout Britain and overseas despite

the fact that he never qualified as an architect. During his illustrious career, Matcham designed around 80 theatres (the majority of them now destroyed). His London theatres include the Coliseum (home of the English National Opera), the Hackney Empire, the Victoria Palace Theatre and the London Palladium.

- Until the 1840s, only certain named theatres – known as "patent theatres" and owned by the most wealthy and influential actor-managers – were permitted to perform drama. Following the passing of the Theatres Act in 1843, these no longer held all the power: entrepreneurs began to build new theatres all over London, spreading from the West End out into the new suburbs.

- Many small and fringe theatres grew out of the Theatre Act of 1843. The Act forbade sale of alcohol in theatres – but permitted it in what would become known as music halls. Many of these remain music venues today, including the Brixton Academy and the Shepherd's Bush Empire. Others, such as the Empire in Leicester Square, went on to become London's first cinemas.

THEATRE TRIVIA

- Wilton's Music Hall in the East End is the world's oldest surviving music hall.
- There have been four Adelphi theatres on the same site on the Strand: the first was built in 1806; the current theatre dates from the 1930s.
- One of the smallest entertainment venues in London is the Cellar Door underneath Aldwych; it's a Victorian loo converted into a cabaret bar.
- *The Mousetrap* by Agatha Christie is the longest-running play in London, on in the West End continuously since 1952.
- The Jermyn Street Theatre was created in the basement of a Piccadilly restaurant. It opened in 1994 and is the smallest theatre in the West End.

SHAKESPEARE'S GLOBE

In 1970, the American actor Sam Wanamaker set up the Shakespeare's Globe Trust. His dream was to rebuild Shakespeare's Globe Theatre on the banks of the Thames in Southwark, very close to its original site. When Wanamaker died in 1993, the project was under construction. Opened to the public in 1997, it was actually the third Globe Theatre. The first was built in 1599 and burnt down in 1613. The second, built on the site of the original, opened in 1614; after it was closed in the 1640s it was demolished and houses built in its place.

CINEMA

HOW CINEMA CAME TO LONDON

- 1889 – Inventor William Friese-Greene attempts to film moving pictures in London.
- 1895 – Birt Acres and Robert Paul make the first motion picture in Britain, *Incident in Clovelly Cottage*, filmed in front of Acres's home in Barnet.
- 1896 – The Lumière brothers bring their moving pictures to London. On 21 February the Cinématographe was revealed to an audience of 54 people at the Marlborough Hall at Quintin Hogg's Polytechnic Institute.
- 1908 – Pathé film studios invent the newsreel to be shown in cinemas; Charles Pathé brings it to London in 1910.
- 1915 – Lime Grove Studios is built in Shepherd's Bush by the Gaumont Film Company.

LONDON FACTS

In 1909, the Palais de Luxe cinema was opened on Great Windmill Street in Soho; later it became the Windmill Theatre.

QUIRKY AND HISTORIC LONDON CINEMAS

- The Barbican Cinema, Barbican
- BFI (British Film Institute), Southbank
- Cine Lumière, Kensington
- Curzon Bloomsbury (formerly Renoir)
- The Electric Cinema, Portobello
- The Gate Picturehouse, Notting Hill
- Genesis, Whitechapel
- The ICA (Institute of Contemporary Arts)
- The Lexi, Kensal Rise
- Phoenix Cinema, East Finchley
- Prince Charles Cinema, Leicester Square
- Rich Mix, Shoreditch

- Rio Cinema, Dalston
- Screen on the Green, Islington
- The Ritzy, Brixton
- Tricycle Cinema (and Theatre), Kilburn

LONDON FACTS

In 2015, the Regent Street cinema opened its doors after refurbishment to its original state – the cinema is inside what is now the University of Westminster but was in 1896 the Polytechnic. The Regent Street cinema was the very first place in London to screen a film.

LONDON ON FILM

Ever since the birth of cinema, London has been a popular filming venue and regularly ranks in the top five film-production destinations in the world. In addition to ubiquitous appearances in the Harry Potter and James Bond franchises, below is a selection of films in which London plays an iconic role:

- *101 Dalmatians*
- *A Clockwork Orange*
- *Absolute Beginners*
- *Alfie*
- *An American Werewolf in London*
- *The Bourne Ultimatum*
- *Bridget Jones's Diary*
- *Brief Encounter*
- *Closer*
- *The Elephant Man*
- *Finding Neverland*
- *Four Weddings and a Funeral*
- *Georgy Girl*
- *The Italian Job*
- *The Lavender Hill Mob*
- *Lock, Stock and Two Smoking Barrels*

- *Love Actually*
- *Match Point*
- *Mona Lisa*
- *Mr Holmes*
- *My Beautiful Launderette*
- *My Week with Marilyn*
- *Notes on a Scandal*
- *Notting Hill*
- *Passport to Pimlico*
- *Quadrophenia*
- *Sliding Doors*
- *Topsy Turvy*
- *Truly, Madly, Deeply*
- *Vera Drake*
- *Withnail and I*

LONDON FACTS

One of the most famous films about London is *Mary Poppins* (1964), but tourists hoping to visit the locations in England will be disappointed. Even though *Mary Poppins* features multiple London locations, it was filmed entirely in the Walt Disney Studios in California.

MUSIC HALLS

By the early nineteenth century, London pubs and taverns had started to offer entertainment, usually singers or singalongs which the drinkers joined in. As the singers grew in popularity, and people came specifically to hear them, pubs started to turn rooms into performance spaces and charge a modest entry fee. The popularity of music hall continued throughout the century, but audience numbers declined steadily in the early twentieth century, not helped by a 1914 law which forbade eating and drinking in theatre auditoriums. The death knell for the music hall was sounded by the arrival of mass cinema. By the 1930s, many music halls were being turned into cinemas; others were demolished.

THE MUSIC HALL THAT INSPIRED AN ARTIST

One of the most popular music halls in the late nineteenth century was The Bedford in Camden. It opened in September 1861, alongside the Bedford Arms pub (on the Duke of Bedford's estate), with an auditorium capacity of nearly 1,200 people. Many of its stars became nationally famous. The Bedford was destroyed in the 1890s and rebuilt as the Bedford Theatre (usually known as "the new Bedford"). It closed its doors for the last time in 1959. One of its regular visitors was the artist Walter Sickert, who was inspired there to paint a number of his most famous works, including *Minnie Cunningham at the Old Bedford* (1892) and *The New Bedford* (*c*.1914–15).

> *A Plea for the Condemned Music Halls*
> *Mr Raymond Blathwayt writes: "May I not urge that the condemned music-halls be spared?… For consider, one of these music-halls may be the one bright spot in a terribly dark neighbourhood; it can either be its greatest curse or almost its supremest blessing. Let the proprietors learn that it is their duty to cater, not for a low, vulgar filthy-minded minority, but for a startling majority of those who desire only that which is highest, and noblest, and best."*
>
> **Pall Mall Gazette**, Tuesday, 15 October 1889

FORMER MUSIC HALLS

- The Coal Hole (on the Strand)
- Shepherd's Bush Empire (O2)
- Hoxton Hall
- Palace Theatre
- Brixton Academy
- Charing Cross Theatre
- Hippodrome

LONDON FACTS

The Shepherd's Bush Empire was designed by legendary theatre architect Frank Matcham and opened as a music hall in 1903. In the 1950s it was reborn as a BBC television studio. In the early 1990s, it was sold by the BBC and became a music venue again.

MUSIC HALL FACTS

- The Cambridge Music Hall in Shoreditch opened in 1864; previously the building had been a synagogue. In the 1890s, it was destroyed by fire and rebuilt. In the 1930s, a tobacco factory was built in its place.
- The Borough Music Hall in Southwark burnt down twice: in 1871 and 1883. It was such a popular venue that it was quickly rebuilt both times.
- The Hippodrome in Leicester Square was specifically designed to be big enough to allow music hall acts by equestrian performers.
- In January 1907, a major strike took place over the poor wages paid to music hall workers. Among those who joined the picket lines were star performers Marie Lloyd and Arthur Roberts. The strike lasted for two weeks and became known as the Music Hall War.
- In 1912, the first Royal Variety Show took place at the Palace Theatre, attended by King George V and Queen Mary. This royal recognition gave a huge boost to music hall and its performers.
- In the late 1920s, Peter Sellers lived above The Bedford with his mother (a stage performer) and grandmother, after his father left them.

PUBS, INNS, TAVERNS AND GIN PALACES

In 1393, King Richard II decreed that all inns in London must have a sign; landlords who refused to put up a sign would "forfeit their ale". Soon pub signs became an invaluable way of mapping the city. London came to be famous for its pubs, many of which have a history that stretches back centuries. In the days before railways and well-maintained roads, coaching inns or taverns (the ancestor of many modern pubs) were a vital part of the transport system. They provided food, water and stabling for exhausted coach horses, as well as food, drink and beds for weary travellers. At a coaching inn, a coach driver could swap his tired horses for fresh ones, and on the return journey exchange them again.

In the nineteenth century, a new type of pub appeared, a place of entertainment and relaxation, richly decorated and intended to seduce passers-by to enter. The combination of lavish decoration and cheap liquor led to the nickname "gin palaces". Two of the most famous extant gin palaces in London are the Princess Louise on High Holborn and Crocker's Folly in St John's Wood.

HISTORIC LONDON PUBS

- The Anchor (London Bridge)
- The Bell (Monument)
- The Cittie of Yorke (Chancery Lane)
- The Crown Tavern (Farringdon)
- The Dove (Hammersmith)
- The Eagle (Old Street)
- The George Inn (London Bridge)
- The George & Vulture (Monument)
- The Grapes (Monument)
- The Guinea (Bond Street)
- Hand & Shears (Barbican)
- The Hoop & Grapes (Aldgate)
- Jack Straw's Castle (Hampstead)
- Jamaica Wine House (Bank)
- The Lamb & Flag (Leicester Square/Covent Garden)
- The Old Bell Tavern (Blackfriars)
- The Old Bull & Bush (Golders Green)
- Ye Olde Cheshire Cheese (Blackfriars)
- Ye Olde Mitre (Chancery Lane)
- The Princess Louise (Holborn)
- The Prospect of Whitby (Wapping)
- Seven Stars (Holborn)
- The Spaniards Inn (Hampstead)
- The Ten Bells (Liverpool Street)
- The White Cross (Richmond)
- The White Hart (Holborn)

LONDON PUB FACTS

- A number of pubs claim to be London's oldest. The George Inn in Southwark, the Cittie of Yorke in Holborn and The Guinea in Bruton Place all date back to the 1400s – but all have been rebuilt.
- Ye Olde Watling pub in the City is believed to have been designed and then used as an office by Sir Christopher Wren while he was working on St Paul's Cathedral; it was also used by his workmen.
- The Mayflower in Rotherhithe was previously known as The Shippe. It was renamed after the ship in which Puritan pilgrims sailed for America,

because the *Mayflower* was moored outside the pub so that its London passengers could embark.

- The Prospect of Whitby in Wapping was formerly known as The Devil's Tavern and said to be the haunt of smugglers and body snatchers.
- The Lamb & Flag pub in Covent Garden dates back to the seventeenth century. The poet John Dryden used to drink here – and reported narrowly escaping death when walking to the pub, which was close to what was then a dangerous slum area. Charles Dickens was also a regular: he had an office on nearby Wellington Street.
- In 1722, the brewer Ralph Harwood claimed to have invented a new drink, known as Porter, at the Bell Brewhouse in Shoreditch.
- Mobile phones are banned in several historic pubs, including The Nag's Head in Knightsbridge.
- The Grenadier pub on Wilton Row is rumoured to be haunted by the ghost of the Duke of Wellington.
- In 1852, there were 38 pubs on Oxford Street alone.
- During World War II, The French House in Soho was a meeting place for French Résistance fighters.
- Writer George Orwell was a regular at the Dog and Duck in Soho.
- The Princess Louise in Holborn opened in 1872, named after Queen Victoria's daughter, a sculptor who enjoyed a Bohemian lifestyle.
- The Blackfriar is an Art Nouveau pub opened in 1905 on the site of the old Blackfriars friary; when it came under threat of demolition the poet John Betjeman stepped in to save it.
- The Freemasons Arms in Hampstead has a skittles alley in the basement.
- The Star Tavern in Belgravia gained notoriety in the mid-twentieth century, when it was revealed as the place where the Great Train Robbers had gathered to plot their attack on a Royal Mail train in 1963. The gang got away with around £2.5 million – and left two railway workers severely beaten and traumatized.
- The Eagle pub near Old Street station stands on the same site as the earlier Eagle Tavern mentioned in "Pop Goes the Weasel":

> *Up and down the City Road,*
> *In and out the Eagle,*
> *That's the way the money goes,*
> *Pop goes the weasel.*

FAMOUS LONDONERS

It is thanks to the poet and conservationist **John Betjeman** that many of London's historic buildings survive. Born in Highgate, on 28 August 1906, an only child, he went to school in Highgate and Oxford, then to university in Oxford – where he clashed with his tutor, C.S. Lewis, and left without finishing his degree. He became a schoolteacher and then a journalist before his first volume of poetry was published in 1931. He also wrote a book on architecture, *Ghastly Good Taste* (1934). In the 1930s he worked in Dublin, as a press officer – and was erroneously believed by some IRA leaders to be a spy. According to legend, when they read his poetry, much of which was scathing about British society, they decided he was not spy material and took him off the assassination list. Betjeman was a founding member of the Victorian Society, which campaigns for the preservation of Victorian architecture. He was knighted in 1969 and made Poet Laureate in 1972. In 1973, he wrote a film, *Metroland*, which celebrated the Metropolitan Railway (much of which is now the Metropolitan Tube line) and the suburbs it served. He died on 19 May 1984, in Trebetherick in Cornwall. One of the successful protests led by Betjeman was against the destruction of St Pancras station (he had been infuriated by the demolition of the 21-m [70-ft] grand arch of Euston station by the British Railways Board in 1962). When St Pancras reopened in 2007, it honoured the poet with the naming of its pub, The Betjeman Arms, and with a larger-than-lifesize bronze statue of Betjeman by sculptor Martin Jennings.

PUBS AND THE RUSSIAN REVOLUTION

- Karl Marx drafted his *Communist Manifesto* in a room above Soho's The Red Lion on Great Windmill Street.
- The Crown Tavern in Clerkenwell – then still known by its original name, The Crown & Anchor – was a favourite drinking haunt of the Russian revolutionary leader Vladimir Lenin when he was living in London. In 1905, Lenin had a meeting at The Crown & Anchor with Joseph Stalin.

LONDON FASHION WEEK

The first London Fashion Week was held in 1984 at Olympia. Organized by the British Fashion Council, it helped make some of its earliest fashion houses and designers, including Ghost and John Galliano, into household names. When Princess Diana attended in 1990, the world began to pay attention, making London one of fashion's "big four" alongside Paris, Milan and New York.

LONDON FASHION WEEK TRIVIA

- London Fashion Week is held twice a year, in February and September.
- In 1984, Katharine Hamnett received its first Designer of the Year award.
- In 1989, a 15-year-old Kate Moss made her first catwalk appearance (for John Galliano).
- In 1992, LFW was held at the Ritz, and included Alexander McQueen's debut collection.
- In 1997, Matthew Williamson's debut collection starred Kate Moss and Jade Jagger on the catwalk.
- In 2007, a new ban ensured no models under the age of 16 were employed in the shows.
- In 2009, London Fashion Week celebrated its twenty-fifth anniversary and was held at Somerset House for the first time.
- In 2012, Men's Fashion Week was launched.

CARNABY STREET

In the late 1960s, the most visited tourist attraction in London was Buckingham Palace; the second-most was Carnaby Street. Until the 1950s, this had been a run-down part of Soho, which meant it offered cheap rent. Fashion shops appeared and soon it became the heart of "Swinging London". The Kinks' song "Dedicated Follower of Fashion" (1966) was written about people who shopped on Carnaby Street. In 1977, Paul Weller wrote "Carnaby Street", but by this time it was no longer the glamorous, fashionable street where The Beatles had shopped. By the 1980s it was seriously in decline, but in the early 2000s it was revamped and by the 2010s was once again a major shopping area, with surrounding streets incorporated into what is now known simply as "Carnaby".

WEMBLEY STADIUM

This entertainment and sporting centre was created for the British Empire exhibition of 1924, but its first event was the 1923 FA Cup Final, held on its opening day, 28 April 1923. The stadium cost £750,000 and was built by Sir Robert McAlpine to a design by Sir John Simpson and Maxwell Ayrton.

- The first piece of turf was cut at the stadium by King George V.
- At the 1923 FA Cup Final, Bolton Wanderers beat West Ham United in front of an estimated 300,000 spectators (the official number allowed was 127,000). The event became known as the "White Horse final" because of the police horse, Billy, who cleared the pitch of invaders.
- The British Empire exhibition took place in 1924 and again in 1925. A new railway line and station was built specially.
- When George V opened the 1924 exhibition, it was the first time his voice was heard on the radio.
- In 1929, speedway rider Fay Taylour won the record for the fastest lap of the Wembley Speedway; she became known as "the Queen of Speedway".
- In 1985, the stadium hosted the Live Aid concert.
- In 2003, in preparation for a new Wembley Stadium, the iconic "twin towers", built in 1923 and 38 m (126 ft) tall, were destroyed.
- In 2006, a new bridge was opened, named White Horse Bridge in honour of the 1923 Cup Final.
- In 2007, a new stadium opened on the same site, seating 90,000.

> *Motor charabancs, as well the new London 'bus services, are likely to cater extensively for visitors to the British Empire Exhibition and for the Cup Tie Final at Wembley Park next April. Arrangements are already being made for bringing large parties of Cup Tie visitors from provincial football centres, direct to the Exhibition grounds…. Cup Tie trippers who wish also to "do London" instead of going direct by rail to one or other of the Wembley stations are arranging to have charabancs to meet parties at the London terminal stations, and to make a tour of the sights of London during Saturday morning, before taking them to the Stadium at Wembley to see the game.*
>
> **Lincolnshire Echo, 9 January 1923**

EARLS COURT EXHIBITION CENTRE

The centre opened in 1887, when one of its first events was the American Exhibition. The Victorian building was replaced in 1937 by a new exhibition centre designed by C. Howard Crane; it had the distinction of being the largest building in Europe made from reinforced concrete. In 2014, the centre was closed, earmarked for demolition.

OLYMPIA

This began life in the nineteenth century, as the National Agricultural Hall, a name which was soon changed. The building, designed by Henry Edward Coe, was famous for its high-arched roof span composed of iron and glass. In 1886, shortly after opening, Olympia staged a circus performance, the "Paris Hippodrome", including a chariot race, and thereafter became known for equestrian events.

O2 ARENA

- The original name of what is now the O2 Arena was the Millennium Dome.
- It was seen as a government failure: an exhibition space intended to show off Britain's achievements at the start of a new millennium – not unlike the Great Exhibition of 1851 – that had attracted a fraction of the visitors expected.
- Against the odds, the Dome was bought and rebranded as a premier entertainment venue.
- In 2012, the O2 – referred to as the North Greenwich Arena – hosted Olympic and Paralympic events.

SOMERSET HOUSE

The first Somerset House, a Tudor palace, was built in the 1540s by the Duke of Somerset – who courted controversy by demolishing a number of buildings, including churches, to use the site. The architecture was quite different from that in London at the time and drew comparisons with Renaissance Italy. The Duke was fated not to enjoy his palace for long: he was executed at the Tower of London, for treason, in 1552. Somerset

House became a royal building, later renamed Denmark House, before being demolished and rebuilt in the 1770s. The new building, once more called Somerset House, was created in the fashionable "classical style". It would later become government offices, naval offices and administration buildings. The Royal Academy was based here until it moved to Piccadilly. For many years the Records Office of births, marriages and deaths was located here. By the 1990s, most administration offices had left and the building became home to art galleries, cafés and restaurants, as well as host of major events including concerts, open-air cinema, London Fashion Week and a winter ice rink.

OPERA HOUSES

In 1732, an opulent new theatre opened on Bow Street in Covent Garden, only to burn down in 1808. A replacement was commissioned from architect Robert Smirke, who also designed the British Museum; a lover of the Greek Revivalist style, he based his theatre on a temple in Athens. It too was destroyed by fire. The 1858 incarnation, however – with recent extensive renovations – is today's **Royal Opera House,** home of the Royal Opera Company and the Royal Ballet. It is often referred to simply as "Covent Garden".

The **Coliseum** is the home of the ENO (English National Opera). The building, designed by Frank Matcham, is the largest theatre in London; it opened in 1904, boasting a revolving stage big enough to house an onstage chariot race. From the 1940s onwards, it was used intermittently and for a while became a cinema. It was renovated in the 1960s and in 1968 reopened as an opera house, for the Sadler's Wells Opera. The company changed its name in the 1970s to the English National Opera. In 2000–04, Matcham's Edwardian theatre was restored to its original glory.

LONDON FACTS

During World War II, the Royal Opera House was a dance hall and the Coliseum was used as a canteen for air-raid wardens.

THE PROMS

- The first Prom took place on 10 August 1895, at the Queen's Hall in Langham Place.
- The name is a shortening of "promenade concerts", because the audience was permitted to walk around.
- The Proms were founded by Robert Newman, manager of the Queen's Hall, together with his new conductor, Henry Wood.
- In the late 1920s, the BBC took over the running of the concerts; Sir Henry Wood (knighted in 1911) was still the conductor.
- In 1941, the Queen's Hall was devastated in a German bombing raid, so the Proms moved to the Royal Albert Hall.
- The Proms remain an annual event at the Royal Albert Hall and on the BBC, with at least 70 main concerts every year.

> *I am going to run nightly concerts to train the public in easy stages, popular at first, gradually raising the standard until I have created a public for classical and modern music.*
>
> **Robert Newman to Henry Wood in 1894**

NOTTING HILL CARNIVAL

The first carnival happened in 1959, and was very different from the multicultural mass celebration it is today. In 1959, it was held inside St Pancras Town Hall, in reaction to the Notting Hill race riots of 1958. The organizer was the Trinidadian political activist and journalist Claudia Jones, who lived in Brixton. She was the editor of Britain's first black weekly newspaper, *The West Indian Gazette*. The carnival soon moved to Notting Hill and became an annual event; the first carnival had been held in winter, to coincide with the dates carnival is celebrated in the Caribbean, but as the weather in London was so cold, it was soon moved to August Bank Holiday weekend. It is alleged that the Notting Hill Carnival was the very first time that a steel band played in public in Britain. The first outdoor carnival was held in 1966, promoted by Claudia Jones, local social worker Rhaune Laslett, political activists and teachers as a way of fostering cultural unity in London.

LONDON FACTS

There is a webcam that looks onto the famous zebra crossing used by The Beatles on Abbey Road (in St John's Wood, just north of Regent's Park). This means visitors can tell their friends amd family all over the world what time they'll be there and then wave to them as they cross.

LONDON EYE

Otherwise known as the Millennium Wheel, the tallest cantilevered observation wheel in the world is 135 m (442 ft) tall; on a clear day, it is possible to see as far as Windsor Castle in Berkshire. The main architects were husband-and-wife team Julia Barfield and David Marks. There are 32 capsules, or "pods", which represent the 32 boroughs of London – but in a nod to superstition, there is no number 13. Pods can be hired for special events, including weddings. In December 2005, the London Eye hosted its first same-sex civil partnership and its lights were turned pink in honour of the celebration.

3

HISTORIC BUILDINGS AND AREAS

THE TOWER OF LONDON

The story of the Tower of London dates back over a millennium, to the arrival of William the Conqueror in 1066. He had several defensive towers built around the city, but the only one surviving today is the White Tower – at the time the tallest building in London, visible for miles – around which the rest of the Tower of London was built over ensuing centuries.

Almost every successive monarch added improvements and extensions, up to the nineteenth century. It is likely that the first monarch to decide to keep a menagerie there was King John, in the twelfth century. Animals included lions, elephants and bears. In the thirteenth century, King Edward I greatly extended the Tower, turning it into one of the most heavily fortified buildings in Europe. He filled in the original moat and built a much deeper one around the new walls.

In Tudor times, Henry VIII became infamous for keeping prisoner and then executing many of his perceived enemies, including two of his wives, at the Tower. Elizabeth I also used the Tower as a prison, even though she herself had been imprisoned there. During the Civil War, it was taken by the Parliamentarians, and Oliver Cromwell caused horror when he ordered the Crown Jewels to be broken down and the components sold to raise money for his cause.

Following the Restoration of the monarchy in 1660, the Tower never regained its formidable reputation as a prison, and gradually became more concerned with royal administration. By the nineteenth century it was revered as a historic monument and began to be opened as a tourist attraction. It still retained some military uses, however, and for 26 years (1826–52) the Constable of the Tower was the Duke of Wellington.

TOWER OF LONDON FACTS

- The first prisoner held at the Tower was Bishop Ranulf Flambard, in 1100; he was also the first person to escape from the Tower (by getting his guards drunk).
- The Tower was not a general prison: it was reserved for those accused of treason.
- In the thirteenth century, part of the Tower's wall collapsed. Religious people believed it was a judgement from God against the King.
- In 1554, the future Elizabeth I was held prisoner at the Tower by her half-sister Queen Mary. This was doubly cruel as the Tower was where Elizabeth's mother, Anne Boleyn, had been executed.
- A total of 22 executions have taken place at the Tower of London.
- The last person executed on Tower Hill was Sir Simon Fraser, Lord Lovat, in 1747; he had been found guilty of involvement in the Jacobite Rebellion.
- On the day of Lord Lovat's execution, 20 spectators were killed by a collapsing scaffold.
- The "execution site" that tourists visit today is a modern invention. There was no single execution site.
- Some of the Tower's oldest walls are 4.5 m (15 ft) thick.
- The first Yeoman Warders arrived at the Tower of London in the thirteenth century, during the reign of Edward IV.
- In 1483, the 12-year-old King Edward V and his little brother Richard of York disappeared from the Tower.
- It is believed that the nickname "Beefeater", for the Yeoman Warders, derives from their privileged position of being provided by the royal chef with as much beef as they wanted to eat, at a time when the meat was very expensive and scarce.
- In the seventeenth century the skeletons of two boys were discovered. They were believed to be the two "Princes in the Tower", as they had become known to history.
- In 1716, a Jacobite prisoner named Lord Nithsdale escaped by dressing up as his wife's maid.

- There was a Royal Mint inside the Tower until the nineteenth century.
- The last person to be executed at the Tower was Josef Jakobs, a German spy, shot by firing squad on 15 August 1941.
- In 2007, Moira Cameron was appointed the first female Yeoman Warder.

TRAITORS' GATE

The river entrance to the Tower of London underneath St Thomas's Tower became known as the Traitors' Gate as prisoners were transported through it.

LONDON FACTS

Legend says that if the ravens ever leave, the Tower of London will crumble. Popular myth claims this saying dates back to the reign of King Charles II – but the facts suggest that the first time it was heard was actually just after World War II. The ravens have their own Yeoman Warder, whose job title is Ravenmaster.

LONDON FACTS

There are four UNESCO World Heritage Sites in London:

- The Tower of London
- Westminster Palace and its churches
- The Royal Botanic Gardens at Kew
- Maritime Greenwich

NO. 1 LONDON

Between 1771 and 1778, a grand house, designed by Robert Adam, was built at Hyde Park Corner. Its first owner was the Earl of Bathurst, but it became famous as the home of the Wellesley family (after 1807), most notably Arthur Wellesley, the first Duke of Wellington.

Although best known as Apsley House (today it is open to the public), its official address is No.1 London. This is because, at the time it was built, it was at the boundary of London. Beyond lay the village of Knightsbridge, and between Apsley House and Knightsbridge was a tollgate. Apsley House was, therefore, the first house in London when riding into the city from the west.

BANK OF ENGLAND

The idea for the Bank of England came from a Scotsman, William Patterson. It was founded in 1694 on Cheapside – inside a hall belonging to the Mercers' Company. The Bank began acquiring land and moved to Threadneedle Street in 1734. The first Bank building there was designed by architect George Sampson in 1732–34; it was extended by Sir Robert Taylor up to 1788, and then remodelled by Sir John Soane, who worked on it for 45 years. Virtually unchanged thereafter for nearly a century, Soane's building was demolished in 1925. Sir Herbert Baker then spent 14 years creating a new bank on the same site. This was completed in 1939, enlarged from three storeys to 10 – although three of those floors are underground. The bank is also home to a free museum.

BANQUETING HOUSE

This is the only building that survives from what was the Whitehall Palace, destroyed by a series of fires. It was a splendid palace, designed by Inigo Jones and decorated with artworks by Peter Paul Rubens and Hans Holbein. The Banqueting House was the site of the execution of Charles I in 1649; contemporary accounts spoke of stunned spectators, shocked at the sight of the regicide. It was also the site of the Restoration of the monarchy in 1660, with the triumphal return of Charles I's son to be crowned King Charles II.

LONDON FACTS

Whitehall's Banqueting House possesses the only ceiling painted by Rubens still in its original site.

CUSTOM HOUSE

- The first recorded custom house in London, where duty on wool was collected, was built in the thirteenth century beside the River Thames at Old Wool Quay, near the Tower of London.
- It was extended and rebuilt several times, until it burnt down in the Great Fire of London.
- Sir Christopher Wren designed a new custom house, finished in 1671, but in 1714 it was severely damaged when a consignment of gunpowder exploded.
- Today's Custom House, on what is now Lower Thames Street, dates from the nineteenth and twentieth centuries; the East Wing was rebuilt after being bombed in World War II.

CHARTERHOUSE

In the 1340s, a wealthy French soldier, who had come to England as a royal servant, bought some land that had been used as a burial site in the Black Death. On it he commissioned a Carthusian priory in 1371, where he was later buried. In 1537, during Henry VIII's dissolution of the monasteries, the Charterhouse was transformed into a Tudor mansion. It was here that both Elizabeth I and James I (of England) first held Court, and that Oliver Cromwell's widow and daughter sought shelter while the monarchy was being restored. In 1611, the mansion was sold to a philanthropist, Thomas Sutton, said to be the wealthiest commoner in Britain. In his will, he left money to save the chapel and turn the buildings into a charitable school and an almshouse, at which the boys and men who were cared for were to be known as Brothers. By the nineteenth century, Charterhouse had become an exclusive fee-paying school, but the governors still provide financial support for scholarships, in line with Thomas Sutton's bequest, and the almshouse continued as a charity. It was at the school that some of the key rules of association football were established, including the off-side rule. Famous former pupils include the Victorian novelist William Thackeray (1811–63). The school moved to Surrey in 1872, but the Charterhouse (sometimes called Sutton's Hospital) remains a home for Brothers. Some of the buildings were damaged during the two world wars, but much of the original medieval buildings survives. Tours of the gardens are held regularly.

CHINATOWN

The first Chinatown in London was in Limehouse in the East End, near the docks where immigrants began their new lives. After World War II, Limehouse was so scarred from the Blitz that the Chinese community began to move out of the area. By the 1950s, there were already several Chinese restaurants on Gerrard Street near Leicester Square. Soon this area had become the new Chinatown.

BARBICAN

London's best-known example of Brutalist architecture was built on 2.2 ha (5.5 acres) of land whose buildings had been destroyed by World War II bombs. Opened by Queen Elizabeth II in 1982 as the Barbican Centre for Arts and Conferences, it houses theatres, cinemas, a library, art galleries and conference facilities. It also has residential tower blocks of purpose-built flats accommodating 6,500 people. The entire complex is Grade II listed.

HAMPTON COURT PALACE

Before it became a royal palace, Hampton Court was the home of Thomas Wolsey, chief minister to Henry VIII. In 1514, the King took it from the disgraced Wolsey and turned it into his own home, of which he was immensely proud. The palace is famous for the gardens with their maze and for the vast Tudor-era kitchens, which demonstrate what life would have been like in Tudor times.

KENSINGTON PALACE

In 1689, the asthmatic King William and his wife Queen Mary bought a country residence outside London, to escape from the unhealthy city air around St James's Palace. Their new home was a Jacobean mansion in the village of Kensington, Nottingham House, which they commissioned Sir Christopher Wren and his assistant Nicholas Hawksmoor to improve. Mary's sister, Queen Anne, then landscaped the gardens and commissioned the Orangery; George I introduced decorations by William Kent. George II spent much of his reign at Kensington but changed it very little, and from the reign of George III onwards, it was no longer a prominent royal residence, instead being given over mostly to minor royals and grace-and-favour apartments. Queen Victoria spent her childhood at the palace and was told of her uncle King William IV's death and her own accession to the throne there in the middle of the night.

FAMOUS RESIDENTS OF KENSINGTON PALACE

- Princess Louise, Duchess of Argyll
- Princess Beatrice of Battenberg
- Princess Margaret and Lord Snowdon
- Diana, Princess of Wales
- Duke and Duchess of Cambridge and their children

BUCKINGHAM PALACE

- The palace was built on a site that had been mulberry orchards.
- Originally known as Buckingham House, it was built for the Tory MP the Duke of Buckingham.
- It was bought by King George III in 1761, but his official home remained St James's Palace. George's wife, Queen Charlotte, gave birth to 14 of their 15 children here.
- During the reign of George IV, the architect John Nash was commissioned to renovate the house and turn it into a palace fit for a monarch, but the King did not move in.
- The first monarch to make the palace their official home was Queen Victoria. It remains the reigning monarch's official London residence.
- The Marble Arch, designed by John Nash, was once attached to the palace, but Queen Victoria asked for it to be removed.
- Electricity was installed in the 1880s.
- The garden covers more than 16 ha (40 acres), encompassing a lake and a helicopter landing pad.
- There are 775 rooms, including 52 royal and guest bedrooms and 188 bedrooms for staff.
- The palace has its own Post Office, chapel, swimming pool and cinema.
- It has a unique postcode: SW1A 1AA

THE ROYAL EXCHANGE

The area around Lombard Street evolved in an attempt to create something like the ancient Roman Forum – a place where businessmen would gather to talk about work and conduct business. Unfortunately, inclement weather often made this cold and unpleasant, and a building was needed for such transactions. The first Royal Exchange building was designed by Thomas Gresham and opened by Elizabeth I in 1571; it was burnt down by the Great Fire of London. The new building survived from 1669 until 1838, when it also burnt down. The current building, designed by William Tite, opened in 1844. It has Grade I listed status and its renovation in the early 2000s had to be consistent with its Victorian history.

THE HOUSES OF PARLIAMENT

Otherwise known as the Palace of Westminster, the Houses of Parliament date back to the eleventh century and the reign of King Cnut. The oldest part of the current buildings is the eleventh-century Westminster Hall; the rest is from the early Victorian period. In 1834, almost all of the original Palace of Westminster burnt to the ground in a catastrophic fire, which raged for days and could be seen for miles around, attracting thousands of horrified onlookers. One of them was the artist J.M.W. Turner (1777–1851), who, like many others, rented a boat to watch it. He exhibited *The Burning of the Houses of Lords and Commons, October 16, 1834*, in 1835. A competition for an architect for the new Houses of Parliament was won by Charles Barry, with interiors designed by Augustus Welby Pugin. The buildings were completed in 1870, but neither man saw his designs brought to life. Pugin died in 1852. Eight years later, Charles Barry died.

BURLINGTON ARCADE

This was once an uncovered alleyway that ran alongside the grounds of Burlington House – which is now the Royal Academy, but in the early nineteenth century was the private home of Lord George Cavendish. According to legend, Cavendish grew so tired of people throwing their rubbish from the alley into his garden that he commissioned an architect to turn it into a covered parade of elegant shops. His declared reason for the project was "for the gratification of the public" and to provide employment in the shops for "industrious females".

ROYAL ALBERT HALL

After the Great Exhibition of 1851, South Kensington (also known as Brompton) began to be developed. Prince Albert had purchased land on which he planned concert halls and museums on the site of a former grand home, Gore House. The nickname for this development was "Albertopolis". Queen Victoria laid the foundation stone for the concert hall on 20 May 1867. She asked that it be named after her dead husband: "The Royal Albert Hall of Arts & Sciences". The first concert was held on 25 February 1871 – but the official opening ceremony by the Prince of Wales (the future Edward VII) was not until 29 March 1871. The foundation stone is under seat 87 in row 11 in the K stalls of the auditorium.

THE ROUNDHOUSE

This venue began life in 1847 as a Victorian railway repair shed, designed by engineer Robert Dockray. By the 1960s it had fallen into disrepair, and the idea was born to turn it into an arts centre. Through the 1970s it gained a reputation for avant-garde and controversial theatre, and Punk gigs, but it closed in 1983 and its future looked rocky. In 2004, it underwent an ambitious renovation by architects John McAslan & Partners, and reopened in 2006 as a venue for all kinds of performance.

ROYAL HOSPITAL, CHELSEA

In 1681, King Charles II issued a royal warrant to build a hospital for impoverished, elderly, ill or disabled soldiers. It was designed by Sir Christopher Wren in what was then rural riverside Chelsea. The first "Chelsea Pensioners" moved in in 1692; the Royal Hospital has remained on the same site ever since, although parts of the building were damaged in both world wars. In 1913, the first Chelsea Flower Show was held in its grounds. Chelsea Pensioners can still be seen walking around London in their distinctive military-style scarlet frock coats (they also have a blue uniform). In 2009, women were accepted for the first time. Prospective Chelsea Pensioners have to fulfil the following criteria: "Anyone who is over 65 and has served as a regular soldier [for at least 12 years], who has no dependent spouse or family, who finds themselves in need and who is 'of good character'."

OLD ROYAL NAVAL COLLEGE, GREENWICH

In the fifteenth century, Margaret of Anjou (wife of Henry VI) bought this site, to turn its manor house into a "palace of pleasaunce". When Henry VIII came to the throne, he created Greenwich Palace, a magnificent home by the river, surrounded by parkland. The splendid palace was devastated, however, during the Civil War; today only its foundations exist. Charles II called in his favourite architect, Sir Christopher Wren, to build on the site, and the work was overseen by Wren's protégé Nicholas Hawksmoor. It became a royal hospital for naval pensioners, then a naval college, and remained a Navy building until 1997, when it was opened to the public.

GREENWICH OBSERVATORY

- The home of Greenwich Mean Time (GMT) and the Prime Meridian line, at Longitude O° O' O".
- Founded by Charles II in 1675.
- Designed by Sir Christopher Wren.
- Named as a UNESCO World Heritage Site in 1997.
- Now owned by the National Maritime Museum and open to the public.

GUILDHALL

There has been a Guildhall in the City of London since the twelfth century. The present building was begun in 1411 and regularly added to until the twentieth century. During the Great Fire, the main part of the building survived when many surrounding buildings and the Guildhall's roofs were destroyed. In 1667, an eyewitness described the scene in his pamphlet *God's Terrible Voice in the City*: "The sight of Guildhall was a fearful spectacle, which stood the whole body of it together in view for several hours together, after the fire had taken it, without flames (I suppose because the timber was such solid oake), like a bright shining coal, as if it had been a palace of gold, or a great building of burnished brass."

OLD BAILEY

The Old Bailey is London's Central Criminal Court. The first building, completed in 1785, was built near Newgate Prison. The new courthouse took its name from the street next to the prison. In 1824, a second courtroom was added, but by the end of the nineteenth century, the building was still deemed too small. Work began on a new Old Bailey in 1902; it was completed in 1907. This building has twice needed repairing after bomb damage: after an air raid in 1941 and an IRA bomb in 1973.

TEMPLE BAR

For 20 years the Temple Bar, designed by Sir Christopher Wren, marked the entrance to the City of London (where The Strand meets Fleet Street). The first mention of a Temple Bar dates back to the 1290s – it probably was an actual bar, preventing people from entering the legal area of London known as "the Temple". In medieval London, the Temple Bar was a proper gateway with a prison cell above it. Wren's Temple Bar was built of fashionable Portland Stone from the royal quarries in Dorset, following the Great Fire. In the 1870s, when London's roads were widened, the Temple Bar was too restrictive, so it was dismantled, stone by stone, and eventually rebuilt at a private estate in Hertfordshire. In 2004, the Temple Bar was returned to the City of London, to the renovated Paternoster Square.

"THE GHERKIN"

Gherkin-shaped 30 St Mary Axe, designed by architect Norman Foster, is 40 storeys high, with a dome at the top that serves as an observation deck. It was built on the site of the Baltic Exchange Building, destroyed in 1992 by an IRA bomb which killed three people and injured 91.

THE SHARD

Opened in 2013, this became the tallest building in London. For its design, intended to emulate a shard of glass, architect Renzo Piano took inspiration from the elegant Gothic church spires that were once the tallest structures in the city. The Shard is 310 m (1,004 ft) high.

LONDON ARCHITECTS

- George Aitchison (1825–1910)
- Charles Barry (1795–1860)
- William Chambers (1723–96)
- Norman Foster (b.1935)
- Edward William Godwin (1833–86)
- George Gilbert Scott (1811–78)
- Giles Gilbert Scott (1880–1960)
- Nicholas Hawksmoor (1661–1736)
- Inigo Jones (1573–1652)
- Edwin Landseer Lutyens (1869–1944)
- John Nash (1752–1835)
- Joseph Paxton (1801–65)
- Richard Rogers (b.1933)
- Norman Shaw (1831–1912)
- Robert Smirke (1781–1867)
- John Soane (1753–1857)
- Alfred Waterhouse (1830–1905)
- Sir Christopher Wren (1632–1723)

LONDON FACTS

Regent Street and The Regent's Park were part of a grand scheme by the Prince Regent (later George IV) and architect John Nash to make central London as opulent as Paris. The plan was to convert Henry VIII's Marylebone hunting grounds into a park, with elegant streets spanning in all directions and connecting to the prince's home, Carlton House, in St James's. After laying out Regent's Park and Regent Street, the money ran out – and the prince was criticized for spending so much when his country was deep in debt through the war with Napoleonic France and many people were living in abject poverty. There was also criticism of Nash's style; the novelist Maria Edgeworth wrote that she was "properly surprised by the new town that has been built in Regent's Park – and indignant at the plaister statues and horrid, useless domes and pediments crowded with mock sculpture figures which damp and smoke must destroy in a season or two".

4

PLACE NAMES

- **Aldwych** is Anglo-Saxon for "old port", a reminder of when the River Thames was much wider than today. It was the principal port (and a market, many traders selling their goods from boats) until a new one was created inside the walls of the City of London.
- **Barbican** refers to the fortifications of the old City of London.
- Several centuries ago, **Blackfriars** was the site of a monastery whose friars wore black, hooded habits.
- **Bread Street** was filled with bakeries and, in 1302, Edward I decreed that bakers could only sell bread from here, nowhere else.
- **Billingsgate** was originally one of the principal wharves of the city, where fishing vessels would arrive and unload cargo. Later it became the name of London's largest fish market.
- **Brick Lane** was once the site of brick and tile factories.
- In 1791, the 1st Earl Camden began a new housing development, dubbed **Camden Town**. His name soon became used for the borough.
- There was once a large farm at **Chalk Farm**, after which the farmhouse was turned into the Chalk Farm Tavern. The name came not from the presence of chalk but from the ancient manor of Chalcot (dating back at least to the time of Edward I).
- **Cheapside** is a corruption of the word "ceap", an Old English word for "market". This was the site of London's biggest market in medieval times.
- **Earls Court** is named after Earl Warwick and Earl Holland, whose lands adjoined in what was then a small hamlet outside London.
- **Fish Street Hill** was once the main thoroughfare leading to London Bridge, a place where fishmongers gathered to sell their wares. It was mentioned by Shakespeare in *King Henry VI (Part II)*: "Up Fish Street!

Down Saint Magnus' Corner! Kill and knock down! Throw them into the Thames!"

- **Garlick Hill** was the site of a garlic market.
- When outdoor worship was popular, there was a large oak tree in present-day **Gospel Oak** under which people gathered to read the Bible aloud.
- **Lombard Street** was named after the Italian region of Lombardy. In 1290, a royal decree forced all Jews to leave England. This proved problematic for the financial world, so Italian bankers, mostly from Lombardy, were invited to move to London and take up financiers' roles.
- In the 1560s, philanthropist William Lamb funded a project to damn a tributary of the River Fleet, so that the water could be used by local people. This is commemorated in **Lamb's Conduit Street**.
- **Millbank** was named for the mill that once stood here and served Westminster Abbey.
- **Old Jewry** was a Jewish settlement in medieval London.
- **Pall Mall** is named after a French game, *pelle melle*, which Charles II introduced to London. It was played in St James's Park, which borders present-day Pall Mall. **The Mall** also takes its name from *pelle melle*.
- The origins of the name **Piccadilly** are disputed. One claim is that it comes from a type of ruff, known as a "pickadill" or "peccadillo", which was fashionable among dandies at the court of James I.
- **Primrose Hill** was once forested, and covered with primroses.
- **Soho** was largely rural until the eighteenth century. Its name derives from a hunting call, "soho", as it was a favoured royal hunting ground.
- **Swiss Cottage** derives its name from a tollbooth built in the style of a Swiss chalet in the 1840s.
- Marble cladding on the exhibition centre created for the Franco-British Exhibition and 1908 Olympics gave the area the name **White City**.
- **Whitecross Street** is named after the Knights Hospitallers, based here; they marked the boundaries of their land with a white cross.

WALLENBERG PLACE

In 2014 a section of Great Cumberland Place, Marylebone, was renamed Wallenberg Place following the installation of a statue honouring a World War II hero: Raoul Wallenberg, a Swedish diplomat who saved thousands of Jews from the Nazis in Hungary.

5

ART AND MUSEUMS

THE BRITISH MUSEUM

- Opened on 15 January 1759 as a free museum for the general public.
- The collection was founded in 1753, based on the eclectic and valuable collection of Sir Hans Sloane, comprising more than 71,000 items.
- The first museum building had been a private home, Montagu House (on the site of the present museum).
- The building was designed by Robert Smirke in Greek Revivalist style, with additions by his brother, Sydney Smirke.
- The iconic round Reading Room of the library is now an exhibition space, with its original features covered over. In its heyday it welcomed such readers as Karl Marx, Anthony Trollope and Charles Dickens.
- The museum receives approximately 6 million visitors a year.
- In 1997, the library was moved to the new British Library at St Pancras.
- In 2000, the new ceiling of the Great Court was unveiled. Designed by Foster & Partners, it was hailed as success of modern architecture, seamlessly melding old and new.

THE SOUTH KENSINGTON MUSEUMS

After the success of the Great Exhibition of 1851, Prince Albert used the profits to buy 32 ha (80 acres) of land in South Kensington to build museums to extend "the influence of Science and Art upon Productive Industry". The first, temporary, buildings were designed by Albert himself. Evocative of the Crystal Palace, but with corrugated iron instead of glass, and painted with green and white stripes, they were opened as a museum by Queen Victoria in June 1857. Even though they were always intended to be temporary, they were derided and nicknamed the "Brompton Boilers". Initially there was just one museum, the South Kensington Museum. Today there are three:

THE NATURAL HISTORY MUSEUM

- In 1860, it was decided that the British Museum's natural collections be moved to South Kensington.
- The British Museum was running out of space and there was a growing public interest in natural sciences, especially since Charles Darwin had published his theory of evolution in 1859.
- The basis of the collection had come from Sir Hans Sloane and the nineteenth-century naturalist and botanist Sir Joseph Banks.
- Architect Alfred Waterhouse (designer of the Oxford Natural History Museum) chose to use variegated terracotta tiles: he was inspired by Venetian palaces, ancient Romanesque religious buildings and new Gothic Revival architecture.
- Work began on the museum in 1873 and it opened in 1881.
- The museum takes up 1.2 ha (3 acres) – although only a small percentage of the whole collection is on display.
- One of its most famous exhibits is the enormous skeleton of a diplodocus dinosaur, but it is actually a cast, not a real skeleton.
- Today it does not look exactly as it did in the nineteenth century, as some of it was destroyed or damaged by wartime bombs, and rebuilt.

THE SCIENCE MUSEUM

- The first buildings here were created for the International Exhibition of 1862.
- Queen Victoria laid the foundation stone of new buildings in 1899.
- In 1913 the architecture was expanded by Sir Richard Allison (it also has much later additions) but the original design was by Aston Webb.
- Allison's buildings took a long time to complete because of World War I, so the museum was not finished until 1928.
- One of its greatest innovations was the introduction of a "children's gallery" in 1931, to encourage children to take up a scientific career.
- In 1949, after World War II, the remaining buildings from 1862 had to be demolished because they were unstable.

- Many of the exhibits came from the Patent Office Museum.
- There are more than 300,000 exhibits.
- Among the many famous items are Stephenson's *Rocket*, Arkwright's "Spinning Jenny", the first electric telegraph and the first jet engine.

FAMOUS LONDONERS

Ada Lovelace (1815–52) was the daughter of the poet Lord Byron and amateur mathematician Annabella (née Milbanke). She barely knew her father, who left his wife a few weeks after Ada was born. Her mother educated Ada in mathematics and science, to a level few women were permitted in that century. Aged 19, she married William King, who was later made Earl of Lovelace (her full title was Lady Ada King, Countess of Lovelace). In 1833, Ada met the computing pioneer Charles Babbage and began working with him. Her groundbreaking work made twentieth-century computing possible and she is often seen as a pioneer of computer software engineering. She died of cancer aged 36. Alan Turing read Ada's work and was inspired by her discoveries.

THE V&A (VICTORIA & ALBERT MUSEUM)

- Dedicated to decorative arts and fashion, the V&A also houses the National Art Library. It covers over 5 ha (12 acres) of land.
- In 1890, a competition was held for a permanent design, offering 300 guineas as the prize. It was won by architect Aston Webb.
- The museum has exhibits from all over the world, including casts of great architectural features such as Trajan's Column from Rome and ancient Greek and Roman statues.
- The V&A has over 4 million exhibits; some are around 3,000 years old.
- It houses the largest collection of Renaissance art outside Italy, the largest collection of Indian art outside India and one of the biggest collections of Islamic art.
- One of its earliest collections came from the Museum of Ornamental Art, which had opened in 1852; it also houses the collection of the School of Design.
- In 1899 Queen Victoria laid the foundation stone of this new museum

and the Science Museum across the road. It was her last important public engagement.
- In memory of her husband, who had died in 1861, she requested the new museum be named the Victoria & Albert Museum.
- By the time it was completed, in 1909, Queen Victoria was also dead. So it was opened by her son, Edward VII.
- The building is made of terracotta brick. Its central tower is 56 m (185 ft) high and was intended to look like a crown.
- The statues of Victoria and Albert above the main doors are by sculptor Alfred Drury.

SOUTH KENSINGTON MUSEUM
This museum is to be opened to the public in June, and arrangements are made with the General Omnibus Company for the conveyance of the public to and from the museum every half hour in the day.

West Middlesex Advertiser and Family Journal, 6 June 1857

LONDON FACTS

The original Brompton Boilers can still be visited: they were moved to Bethnal Green and became incorporated into the Museum of Childhood (which is owned by the V&A).

SOME OF LONDON'S MOST INTERESTING MUSEUMS
- Bank of England Museum
- Bankside Museum
- Black Cultural Archives
- British Dental Association Museum
- British Museum
- British Postal Museum & Archive
- British Red Cross Museum & Archives
- Brunel Museum
- Cartoon Museum
- Churchill War Rooms
- Cinema Museum

- Clink Prison Museum
- Clockmakers' Museum
- Cuming Museum
- Design Museum
- Fan Museum
- Fleming Museum
- Florence Nightingale Museum
- Foundling Museum
- Garden Museum
- Geffrye Museum
- Grant Museum of Zoology
- Horniman Museum
- Household Cavalry Museum
- Hunterian Museum
- Imperial War Museum
- London Fire Brigade Museum
- London Sewing Machine Museum
- London Transport Museum
- Madame Tussaud's
- Magic Circle Museum
- Museum of Brands, Packaging & Advertising
- Museum of Comedy
- Museum of Freemasonry
- Museum of London
- Museum of London Docklands
- Museum of the Order of St John
- National Army Museum
- National Maritime Museum
- Old Operating Theatre Museum
- Petrie Museum
- Pollock's Toy Museum
- Ragged School Museum
- Royal Artillery Museum
- Twinings Museum
- V&A Museum of Childhood
- Vault at the Hard Rock Cafe
- Wellcome Collection

MUSEUM FACTS

- London is home to more than 200 museums and galleries.
- The Twinings Tea Museum is the oldest shop in the City of Westminster still owned by the same family, and is still selling the same products (tea and coffee) as when it opened in 1706.
- The Black Cultural Archives opened in Windrush Square in Brixton in 2014, from a collection founded in 1981. It was the first dedicated black heritage centre in Britain and runs regular exhibitions and events. The centre's collection celebrates the history and heritage of British people of African and Caribbean descent.

HOUSE MUSEUMS

- Benjamin Franklin House
- Carlyle House
- Charles Dickens Museum
- Denis Severs House
- Dr Johnson's House
- Emery Walker House
- Freud Museum
- Handel House
- Hogarth's House
- Keats House
- Leighton House
- Linley Samborne House
- Sherlock Holmes Museum
- Sir John Soane's Museum
- Wesley Chapel & Museum of Methodism
- William Morris Gallery

HISTORIC SHIPS

- *Cutty Sark*
- *Golden Hind*
- HMS *Belfast*

PETRIE MUSEUM

This was opened in 1892 as part of University College London, to teach students about Egyptian archaeology. It is named after William Flanders Petrie, the university's first professor of Egyptology. Today the museum houses around 80,000 objects from the Nile Valley, specializing in Egyptian and Sudanese archaeology from ancient times up to the Islamic period. Its exhibits – mostly collected or overseen by Petrie himself – include 7,000-year-old Egyptian linen, a dancer's dress dating from 2,400 BC, Roman socks and sandals, and a marble relief carving of the fertility god Min, depicted with a huge erect penis.

WIENER LIBRARY

Russell Square is home to one of the world's leading archives on Nazism, the Holocaust and genocide, established by Dr Alfred Wiener, a German Jew who fled Hitler's Germany in 1933. Moving initially to Amsterdam, he founded the Jewish Central Information Office (JCIO) in collaboration with the British Jewish community. In 1938, the Wiener family left for London, bringing the archive with them. The library contains printed materials, official records and personal memories of the Nazi era and anti-Semitism. Its collection proved vital just after World War II, as evidence in the Nuremberg Trials.

RAGGED SCHOOL MUSEUM

Opened in 1990 on the former site of social campaigner Dr Barnardo's first "ragged school" (free primary school for poor children), the Copperfield Road Free School, this museum teaches visitors about the Victorian education system, as well as what life was like in a poor East End home in nineteenth-century London, without running water or electricity.

FOUNDLING MUSEUM

The museum tells the story of the Foundling Hospital children's home in Bloomsbury (founded by Thomas Coram in 1739), in whose former grounds it stands. Thanks to Coram's influential friends, including composer George Handel and artist William Hogarth, the hospital attracted paying visitors to view works by famous artists and listen to concerts of Handel's music; profits went towards the children's food, clothes and education. Almost a century later, the young Charles Dickens was living nearby, at 48 Doughty Street (now the Charles Dickens Museum). He walked past every day and the Foundling Hospital inspired him when writing *Oliver Twist*, the story of an orphaned child. The hospital was demolished in the 1920s but its collection is still displayed here.

FAMOUS LONDONERS

In 1720, **Thomas Coram** (1688–1751), a merchant sailor, returned to London after years at sea and was horrified to see the poverty that forced women to give up their children. At the time, unmarried women would lose their jobs if they were known to have a baby. Coram hated to see how many babies were abandoned or killed. So he set up the Foundling Hospital, a charity to which women could bring their babies to be cared for and educated. It was an amazing, kindly place and today it is remembered by the Foundling Museum and the Coram children's charity.

ARTISTIC FIRSTS

- Coram's Foundling Hospital, opened in 1739, contained London's first public art gallery. Coram's friend the artist William Hogarth donated his own works and persuaded other notable artists, including Joshua Reynolds and Thomas Gainsborough, to do the same. These were displayed inside the hospital and people paid to see them.
- The first purpose-built art gallery in London was the Dulwich Picture Gallery. Construction began in 1811, under architect Sir John Soane. Special features included skylights, to allow maximum hanging space on the walls as well as reducing the risk of light damage to the artworks. A new bespoke paint colour was created to show off the paintings in their gilded frames to best advantage; it became commercially available as Picture Gallery Red. The paintings were moved into the new gallery in 1814, and the following year Royal Academicians and art students were invited to visit. In 1817, the gallery opened to the public.

ART GALLERIES

- Barbican Art Gallery
- Ben Uri Gallery
- Courtauld Gallery
- Dulwich Picture Gallery
- Estorick Collection of Modern Italian Art
- Guildhall Art Gallery
- Institute of Contemporary Arts
- National Gallery
- National Portrait Gallery
- Photographers' Gallery
- Queen's Gallery
- Royal Academy of Arts
- Saatchi Gallery
- Serpentine Gallery
- Tate Britain
- Tate Modern
- Wallace Collection
- Whitechapel Art Gallery

THE ROYAL ACADEMY

During the reign of Elizabeth I the royal court briefly favoured British artists, such as the miniaturist Nicholas Hilliard. But before and after her reign, royalty looked overseas for its court artists, particularly to Germany, Italy and other places with an art academy. By the eighteenth century, it was apparent that something needed to be done, not least because Britain's best artists were leaving the country to train in France, Rome and Antwerp's academies. In 1768, the Royal Academy of Arts was founded, and in 1769 it received its royal charter from George III and opened to students and the public. From the beginning tuition was free for promising artists, as long as their work could pass the exam. Costs were covered by the Summer Exhibition of students' work. Although there were two female founder members – Angelica Kauffman and Mary Moser – no female artists or other female Academicians were admitted until the twentieth century. In 1936, Dame Laura Knight became the first woman elected to the Royal Academy since 1768.

THE FOURTH PLINTH

A contemporary art prize is based around the once-empty plinth in Trafalgar Square. When the square was laid out, the three other plinths were given statues – Major General Sir Henry Havelock, General Napier and King George IV – but the fourth was meant for a statue of King William IV, which was never created. In 1998, the idea of using the plinth to showcase contemporary art was proposed by the Royal Society of Arts.

CANALETTO IN LONDON

The Italian artist Canaletto, most famous for his Venetian scenes, visited England several times during 1746 and 1756. His London paintings include *The River Thames with St Paul's Cathedral on Lord Mayor's Day* (1746), *Westminster Abbey with a Procession of the Knights of the Bath* (1749) and *Northumberland House* (1752). He was a regular visitor to pleasure gardens, painting Ranelagh Gardens in *Interior of the Rotunda at Ranelagh* (1754) and *Vauxhall Gardens in View of the Grand Walk* (1751).

ILLUSTRATING LONDON

Thousands of artists have been inspired by London over the centuries, including:

- Anna Airy (1882–1964)
- Banksy (b.1974)
- Vanessa Bell (1879–1961)
- Robert Bevan (1885–1925)
- Jacques-Emile Blanche (1861–1942)
- John Bratby (1928–92)
- Canaletto (1697–1768)
- Gustave Doré (1832–83)
- Bernard Dunstan (b.1920)
- Luke Fildes (1843–1927)
- William Powell Frith (1819–1909)
- Mark Gertler (1891–1939)
- Harold Gilman (1876–1919)

- Thomas Girtin (1775–1802)
- Duncan Grant (1885–1978)
- Spencer Gore (1878–1914)
- Sylvia Gosse (1881–1968)
- Walter Greaves (1846–1930)
- John Atkinson Grimshaw (1836–93)
- William Hogarth (1697–1764)
- Laura Knight (1877–1970)
- Oskar Kokoschka (1886–1920)
- Leon Kossoff (b.1926)
- William Logsdail (1859–1944)
- William Marlow (1740–1813)
- Claude Monet (1840–1926)
- Balthazar Nebot (active 1730–*c*.1765)
- Grayson Perry (b.1960)
- Camille Pissarro (1830–1903)
- Walter Sickert (1860–1942)
- Ruskin Spear (1911–90)
- Joseph Mallord William Turner (1775–1851)
- Vincent van Gogh (1853–90)
- James Abbott McNeill Whistler (1834–1903)

FAMOUS LONDONERS

The artist **William Hogarth** was born near Smithfield Market. In his teens he was apprenticed to a silversmith engraver, Ellis Gamble; it was vital that he earn money to support his family because his father, Richard Hogarth, was incarcerated in the Fleet debtors' prison. In 1729 he married Jane Thornhill, daughter of his tutor William Thornhill, who ran a successful drawing school which Hogarth later took over. He became renowned for his scenes of London life, for instance *Gin Lane* and *Beer Street*, caricatures and series paintings including *The Rake's Progress*. Hogarth and Jane began married life at a house in Leicester Square, but also bought a country house, now a museum, outside London in the village of Chiswick. Hogarth's name lives on in one of the busiest roundabouts in west London.

6

PARKS AND GARDENS

ROYAL PARKS

There are eight Royal Parks in London, comprising over 2,000 ha (around 5,000 acres) of ancient parkland open to everyone. They are:

- Bushy Park
- The Green Park
- Greenwich Park
- Hyde Park
- Kensington Gardens
- The Regent's Park (including Primrose Hill)
- Richmond Park
- St James's Park

OTHER PARKLAND AND GREEN SPACES

- Barnes Common
- Battersea Park
- Bishop's Park
- Blackheath Common
- Brockwell Park
- Bushy Park
- Camley Street Natural Park
- Clapham Common
- Clissold Park
- Crystal Palace Park

- Ealing Common
- Greenwich Park
- Hampstead Heath
- Harrow Weald Common
- Highgate Wood
- Holland Park
- Lee Valley Park
- London Fields
- Morden Hall Park
- Phoenix Garden
- Postman's Park
- Queen Elizabeth Olympic Park
- Ravenscourt Park
- Royal Botanic Gardens, Kew
- Streatham Common
- Tooting Bec Common
- Victoria Park
- Wandsworth Common
- Wanstead Flats
- Wimbledon Common
- Wormwood Scrubs Park

LONDON'S PLEASURE GARDENS

During the seventeenth and eighteenth centuries, a popular public attraction was "pleasure gardens" – gardens with additional entertainments. There were many small parks given the name pleasure garden by entrepreneurial owners, but only three famous pleasure gardens: Vauxhall, Marylebone and Ranelagh. Ranelagh and Marylebone had closed down by the nineteenth century, and Vauxhall had become considerably shabby, but in the 1840s the Cremorne Pleasure Garden opened in Chelsea. Pleasure gardens were renowned as haunts of prostitutes and pickpockets, and visits to them were not considered suitable for upper- or middle-class women.

- Vauxhall Garden opened in 1661 and was initially known as New Spring Gardens.

- Pleasure gardens were immortalized in many literary works, including Samuel Pepys's diary, John Evelyn's diary, Fanny Burney's *Evelina*, William Thackeray's *Vanity Fair* and John Keats's poem "To a Lady Seen for a Few Moments at Vauxhall".
- The programme for Vauxhall's events during August 1850 included lion-tamers, fortune tellers, ventriloquists, acrobats, dancing horses, fire walkers, monkeys, trampolining clowns and jugglers.

> *We were now arrived at Spring-Garden, which is exquisitely pleasant at this time of the Year. When I considered the Fragrancy of the Walks and Bowers, with the Choirs of Birds that sung upon the Trees, and the loose Tribe of People that walked under their Shades, I could not but look upon the Place as a kind of Mahometan Paradise. Sir Roger told me it put him in mind of a little Coppice by his House in the Country, which his Chaplain used to call an Aviary of Nightingales....*
>
> *As we were going out of the Garden, my old Friend ... told the Mistress of the House, who sat at the Bar, That he should be a better Customer of her Garden, if there were more Nightingales, and fewer Strumpets.*
>
> **Joseph Addison, *The Spectator,* 1712**

HYDE PARK

Covering 140 ha (350 acres) of central London, this was once private parkland for the monks at Westminster Abbey, until Henry VIII appropriated it as his private hunting ground. The first monarch to allow the public to enter – albeit only a privileged few – was James I. It was the ill-fated Charles I who gave the park to his people, making it a public space in 1637, 12 years before his execution. Rotten Row, still popular for riding, was created by William III, who wanted a properly lit path: 300 oil lamps were placed along the route he liked to take to Kensington Palace, making it the country's first lit highway. The name Rotten Row is a corruption of the original French name, *Route du Roi* (road of the king). The park's lake, the Serpentine, was created by Queen Caroline, wife of George II.

KENSINGTON GARDENS

With an area of 98 ha (242 acres), this was once part of Hyde Park, until Queen Caroline requested it be landscaped separately. When it reopened to the public, a strict dress code was required. After Queen Victoria came to the throne in 1837, she added improvements such as the Italian Gardens and the Albert Memorial (to her husband, Prince Albert, who had died in 1861). Statues in the gardens include the famous Peter Pan.

ST JAMES'S PARK

This was once the site of St James's Hospital, which specialized in treatment of female lepers. The women were given the task of caring for pigs, which thrived in the swampy marshland. When Henry VIII took the land, he had it drained and turned into parkland for Whitehall Palace and his new St James's Palace. Charles II ordered the redesign of the park and opened it to the public for the first time. On 18 August 1661, Samuel Pepys wrote in his diary, "So I went to White Hall ... and then to walk in St James's Park, and saw great variety of fowl which I never saw before and so home." In the eighteenth and nineteenth centuries, the park grew smaller: houses, including Buckingham House, were built and the roads became busier and more defined. Today it looks much as it did when John Nash landscaped it during the reign of George IV.

LONDON FACTS

The Royal Parks corporation also manages Victoria Tower Gardens, Brompton Cemetery, Grosvenor Square Garden and the gardens of numbers 10, 11 and 12 Downing Street.

LONDON'S GARDEN SQUARES

- Garden squares were specifically built for residents of the surrounding square.
- In 1931, the London Squares Act was passed, to protect more than

400 garden squares and prevent them being sold off for development.
- Today, some are open to the public, some only at certain times, and others are still accessible only by key-holding residents.
- Open Garden Squares Weekend is an annual event.
- There are a number of garden squares in Bloomsbury; as a result the local clique of artists and writers known as the Bloomsbury Group, who had unconventional private lives, were famously said to "live in squares and love in triangles".

CHELSEA PHYSIC GARDEN

In 1673, the Apothecaries' Garden was founded in Chelsea, as a training garden for apprentice apothecaries. Throughout the following centuries it continued in this role, and from the 1870s included training for women. In 1983, the Chelsea Physic Garden (as it was now known) became a charity and opened to the public.

KING'S CROSS SKIP GARDEN

Since the twenty-first-century regeneration work around King's Cross, a new urban garden has grown up. The Skip Garden is run by the charity Global Generation for young people to come and learn about growing fruit and vegetables, keeping bees for honey and making jam and chutney. The name comes from the fact that the produce – sold to local bars, restaurants and cafés – is grown in skips. The skips can be moved if the garden needs to change its location.

SKY GARDEN

London's highest garden is at 20 Fenchurch Street, on top of the skyscraper known as "The Walkie Talkie" because of its shape. The garden was opened in 2015, inside a glass dome, and offers 360° views.

Green is the plane-tree in the square,
The other trees are brown;
They droop and pine for country air;
The plane-tree loves the town.

Here from my garret-pane, I mark
The plane-tree bud and blow,
Shed her recuperative bark,
And spread her shade below.

Among her branches, in and out,
The city breezes play;
The dun fog wraps her round about;
Above, the smoke curls grey.

Others the country take for choice,
And hold the town in scorn;
But she has listened to the voice
On city breezes borne.

Amy Levy (1861–89), "A London Plane Tree", 1889

LONDON FACTS

In the eighteenth century an area of Wimbledon Common became known as Caesar's Camp. Although there was no proof that the Romans had made camp there, it had been home to a settlement dating back to *c.*700 BC. A second area also named Caesar's Camp was excavated in 1944, at Heathrow. After the excavation, building work continued on the new airport. The archaeological site is now buried beneath one of the runways.

KEW GARDENS

The Royal Botanic Gardens at Kew were once the Royal Family's private parkland for Kew Palace. In 1759, a specialist from Chelsea Physic Garden was hired to work at Kew and start to turn it into another apothecary garden, full of healing and miraculous plants. By the start of the nineteenth century, Kew Palace was little used and the gardens were suffering from lack of funds, but the start of the Victorian era saw new interest in natural sciences and money began to be spent on the gardens again, most notably the creation of the grand Victorian greenhouses, the Palm House and the Temperate House (the latter is the largest Victorian greenhouse in the world). In 1869, the railway was extended as far as Kew and the gardens began to attract many more visitors. They were also used for scientific and botanical research. In July 2003, Kew Gardens was named a UNESCO World Heritage Site. Today, it welcomes over 1.3 million visitors annually.

CEMETERIES

The Romans insisted that all burials take place outside the city walls. In later centuries, Roman burial sites became part of central London, and new cemeteries outside the city were established. In 1999, excavations at Spitalfields uncovered a Roman cemetery. During the Victorian era, death and mourning became almost a cult, as the people followed their queen into extended mourning for her young husband. Cemeteries became lucrative businesses and Victorians vied with each other to produce more and more elaborate gravestones, memorial tombs and family mausoleums.

As the population of London expanded rapidly through the nineteenth century, it became apparent that something had to be done about the ever-growing number of dead Londoners. In 1882, an Act of Parliament was passed, known as the London Cemeteries Act. As a result seven public cemeteries were created in a ring around London, all designed for use as public parks as well as burial grounds:

- Kensal Green (1832)
- Norwood (1837)
- Highgate (1839 West Cemetery; 1854 East Cemetery)
- Nunhead (1840)
- Brompton (1840)
- Abney Park (1840)
- Tower Hamlets (1841)

The design of **Kensal Green** was inspired by the Parisian cemetery of Père Lachaise. It spans 29 ha (72 acres), runs alongside the Grand Union Canal and contains two wildlife conservation areas. Residents include the father-and-son engineers Marc Brunel and Isambard Kingdom Brunel; authors Anthony Trollope, Wilkie Collins, Leigh Hunt and William

Makepeace Thackeray; George III's daughter Princess Sophia; publisher John Murray; chef Alexis Soyer; tightrope walker Emile Blondin (the pseudonym of Jean-François Gravelet); Charles Dickens's teenaged sister-in-law Mary Scott Hogarth (whose death led the author to miss a writing deadline for the only time in his career); royal nanny Mary Ann Thurston (whose monument was carved by one of her charges, Queen Victoria's sculptor daughter Princess Louise); and Dr John Elliotson, who pioneered the use of the stethoscope in medical practice.

LONDON FACTS

In 1884, a change in the law made cremation legal in Britain. London's first crematorium was opened in 1902, at Golders Green. It is set in 5 ha (12 acres) of land opposite the Jewish cemetery and holds monuments to a number of celebrities, including Joyce Grenfell, Marc Bolan, Peter Sellers, Keith Moon, Bram Stoker, Peter Sellers, Shiva Naipaul, Anna Pavlova and Sigmund Freud.

Highgate Cemetery covers 15 ha (37 acres) and is Grade II listed. The architect was Stephen Geary. It is renowned for its grandiose monumental architecture, such as the Egyptain Avenue in the West Cemetery and the Circle of Lebanon, created at a time when excitement about archaeological expeditions to North Africa was at a peak. Over 170,000 people are buried at Highgate. Its many celebrities include: writers Douglas Adams, Christina Rossetti, Karl Marx, George Eliot and Radclyffe Hall; actors Ralph Richardson, Corin Redgrave and Max Wall; artists Lizzie Siddal, Anna Mahler, Edwin Landseer, Feliks Topolski and Patrick Caulfield; scientists Michael Faraday, Andrew Baird and Frederick Pavy; and musicians Bert Jansch, Liza Lehmann, Carl Rosa and Malcolm Maclaren. Other notables include Claudia Jones (activist and founder of the Notting Hill Carnival), Yusuf Dadoo (anti-apartheid activist), Elizabeth Lilley (Queen Victoria's midwife), Paul Foot (investigative journalist) and the murdered Russian political activist Alexander Litvinenko. Among the most-photographed graves are those of Julius Beer, George Wombwell and Thomas Sayer. Beer, an impoverished child who became a newspaper magnate and one of the wealthiest men in Britain, commissioned a grand mausoleum for his family on the highest point in the cemetery. George Wombwell began his career as a cordwainer (a person who made leather goods), but his passion for animals led him to collect a variety of weird and wonderful pets, beginning with a pair of boa constrictors, which he exhibited in public for a fee. On his tomb is carved the word "menagerist", with a sculpture of a slumbering lion. Thomas Sayer was one of the nineteenth century's most famous bare-knuckle boxers. His grave is guarded by a life-size sculpture of his faithful dog, Lion: dressed in a ruff of black mourning crape, the dog was the chief mourner at Sayer's funeral, at which an estimated 10,000 spectators showed up.

Abney Park was created out of two grand estates, the parklands of neighbouring Abney House and Fleetwood House. As well as a cemetery, it was also laid out as an arboretum. Initially, it was known as the graveyard for Nonconformists – those who were not members of the Protestant church. Graves include those of the Booth family (founders of the Salvation Army) and Joanna Vassa (daughter of freed slave and anti-slavery campaigner Olaudah Equiano).

LONDON FACTS

The first cemetery for Dissenters (as Nonconformists were also known) was founded in 1665 at Bunhill Fields, north of the City. Its graves include those of authors John Bunyan and Daniel Defoe, artist-cum-poet William Blake, and Susannah Wesley, mother of Methodist preachers John and Charles Wesley. The cemetery's name derives from "bone hill", redolent of its past as a repository for bones from other graveyards: as a church's graveyard filled up, its old graves would be dug up and the bones thrown away. This is also believed to be the site of a Saxon burial ground.

Brompton Cemetery is Grade I listed and is the UK's only public cemetery to be owned by the monarch. Covering 16 ha (39 acres), it was designed by Benjamin Baud in neoclassical architectural style. Within its grounds are buried suffrage leader Emmeline Pankhurst, cricketer John Wisden, opera singer Blanche Roosevelt, racing driver Percy Lambert (the first person to drive a car at 160 kph/100 mph), Henry Mears (founder of Chelsea Football Club), shipping magnate Samuel Cunard, Pre-Raphaelite artist Charles Allston Collins (brother of Wilkie Collins and husband of Katey Dickens, daughter of Charles Dickens) and groundbreaking medic Dr John Snow, who helped discover the causes of cholera and pioneered the use of chloroform. There is also a grave monument to Native American Sioux chief Long Wolf, but his remains were returned to South Dakota in 1997.

Tower Hamlets Cemetery had the dubious distinction of being bombed five times during World War II. It was closed for burials in 1963, and reopened in 1967 as a public park.

JEWISH CEMETERIES

The oldest known Jewish cemetery in London, established in 1657 on Mile End Road, was Betahayim Velho, also known as the Old Sephardi Cemetery. Twelve years later the first Ashkenazi cemetery was created, on Alderney Road. The New Sephardi Cemetery (also on Mile End Road) dates from 1725, and a second Ashkenazi cemetery, the New Synagogue Burial Ground, came into being on Brady Street. The land had previously been a place for manufacturing bricks, for the thriving building industry. Famous people buried here include Moses Jacob (founder of the New Synagogue); Nathaniel Mayer Victor, 3rd Baron Rothschild; Solomon Herschel, the Chief Rabbi of Britain; and the social campaigner Miriam Levy, who founded the first soup kitchen in impoverished Whitechapel.

LONDON FACTS

One of London's smallest graveyards, Chiswick Old Cemetery (1888), is also a resting place for three of its most renowned artists: James Abbott McNeill Whistler, William Blake Richmond and William Hogarth.

GARDENS OF PEACE

In 2002 the largest Muslim cemetery in the UK was created in London. Three years later, it was the site of the first funeral for a victim of the 7/7 bombings. Shahara Islam, a Muslim Londoner, who worked as a bank cashier, was killed on the number 30 bus when it was targeted by a suicide bomber.

THE NECROPOLIS RAILWAY

When London's cemeteries became too full, a solution further outside the city was found: a new cemetery at Brookwood in Surrey. It opened in 1854, and for a while held the distinction of being the world's biggest. The question of how to transport coffins and mourners the 40 km (25 miles) from London was answered by the creation of the Necropolis Railway. This was a special service from Waterloo, with its own private terminus (now destroyed) by the main station. The Necropolis train first ran on 13 November 1854, and continued, once a day, as long as a funeral was taking place, for over 50 years. It ceased during World War II, and just a couple of years after the war's end, the train lines were removed. Now that most people had access to funeral cars, the Necropolis Railway was no longer needed. Among the many graves at Brookwood are those of artists John Singer Sargent, William de Morgan and Evelyn de Morgan, writer Dame Rebecca West, and Horatia Nelson Johnson, granddaughter of Lord Nelson.

LONDON FACTS

In 2003, *Archaeology* magazine published a report into what looked like the desecration of perhaps London's oldest cemetery. Ancient Roman graves in the City of London are believed to have been destroyed by troops loyal to Queen Boudicca in *c.*AD 61.

MEMORIALS

- London has only two Grade I listed grave memorials: the tombs of Sir John Soane in St Pancras Old Church graveyard and of Karl Marx in Highgate Cemetery. The architect and designer Sir Giles Gilbert Scott was inspired by Soane's tomb when designing the K2 telephone box.
- There are two Kindertransport memorials at Liverpool Street station. These commemorate the children, around 10,000 in total, saved from Nazi Germany by transportation to the UK on special trains between 1938 and 1940. One of the key figures in the rescue of hundreds of children from Czechoslovakia was Hampstead-born Sir Nicholas Winton (1909–2015).

- At 28 St James's Place is a plaque to William Huskisson, a statesman who had the dubious distinction of being the first person in the world killed by a train. He was run over by the *Rocket* on its inaugural journey.
- On Victoria Embankment is a statue to the Imperial Camel Corps, which fought in Sinai and Palestine during World War I.
- The Boer War memorial in St Paul's Cathedral was sculpted by Queen Victoria's daughter Princess Louise. She also made the statue of her mother in Kensington Gardens.
- Opposite the National Portrait Gallery is a statue remembering Edith Cavell, a British nurse working in Brussels in World War I who helped hundreds of Allied soldiers escape. She was shot by the Germans as a spy in 1915.
- At Hyde Park Corner is a memorial to the Royal Artillery. Its bronze figure was sculpted by Charles Sargeant Jagger.
- In Victoria Embankment Gardens is a bronze memorial to Sir Arthur Sullivan (one half of Gilbert & Sullivan), featuring a semi-naked weeping woman. To the general public it was intended to be the muse of music crying over his demise; his friends knew that it was indicative of the many women he had loved, including his grieving mistress at the time of his death.
- In the middle of Park Lane is the poignant Animals in War memorial. It was unveiled in 2004, to mark the ninetieth anniversary of World War I.
- Since 7 July 2009, Hyde Park has contained a memorial consisting of 52 stainless-steel columns. These represent the 52 victims of the Tube and bus bombings on 7 July 2005.
- The stone monument outside Charing Cross station is a nineteenth-century replica of the original Eleanor Cross, which commemorated the funeral journey of the coffin of Eleanor of Castile, wife of Edward I. She died in 1290, and 12 stone "crosses" were erected in her memory around the country. London's Eleanor Cross stood near present-day Charing Cross, at the spot where the equestrian statue of Charles I now stands. It was considered the central point of London and the place from where all milestones were measured.
- A statue to Russia's Peter the Great was unveiled in Deptford in 2001; it commemorates the Tsar's 1698 visit to Deptford, where he rented a house from the diarist John Evelyn.

LONDON FACTS

The Shaftesbury Memorial Statue at Piccadilly Circus is better known as Eros. It was commissioned from sculptor Alfred Gilbert as a memorial to the Victorian philanthropist and campaigner the 7th Earl of Shaftesbury (after whom Shaftesbury Avenue is named). It actually isn't Eros, the Greek god of love, but his brother Anteros, god of requited love. The Victorian public was greatly disturbed by his nudity, so the word was put out that he was "the angel of Christian charity".

BLUE PLAQUES

- The idea of London's commemorative Blue Plaques came about in 1863.
- The first Blue Plaque was to Lord Byron in 1867, on his birthplace in Cavendish Square – but when the house was demolished in 1889, the plaque was destroyed.
- The earliest Blue Plaque still in existence was also erected in 1867; it marks a house where the French emperor, Napoleon III, lived in 1848, in King Street in Westminster.
- The only Blue Plaque in the City of London is to Dr Johnson.
- English Heritage became responsible for the scheme in 1896.
- There are more than 880 Blue Plaques in London alone (as well as similar commemorative plaques that aren't part of the official scheme).
- In Mayfair's Brook Street are two plaques to musicians, side by side: one to George Frideric Handel, the other to Jimi Hendrix.
- The criteria for a Blue Plaque include the person having been dead for at least 20 years and no more than two plaques on one building.

> *"To tell you the God's honest truth, I haven't heard much of the fella's stuff."*
>
> **Jimi Hendrix's reported comment when told he was living next to Handel's former home**

7

CRIME

Like all major cities, London has a long history of crime. Archaeologists have found evidence of crime-prevention measures – such as window bars and locks – on buildings dating back to the Roman occupation, as well as records of crimes carried out.

> *As clever Tom Clinch, while the Rabble was bawling,*
> *Rode stately through Holbourn, to die in his Calling;*
> *He stopt at the George for a Bottle of Sack,*
> *And promis'd to pay for it when he'd come back...*
> **Jonathan Swift, "Clever Tom Clinch, going to be hanged", 1726**

SPRING-HEELED JACK

For decades the people of London were terrorized by the legend of a monster known as Spring-heeled Jack, said to attack people on dark nights before leaping away on unhuman legs so powerful that he could spring onto rooftops or over houses. Gradually the legend came to be taken less seriously by the educated classes. In 1838, the *London Standard* interviewed a police officer who said "that it was his opinion that in consequence of the notoriety which the gambols of 'Spring-heeled Jack' had gained, the character was now associated by many thoughtless young men, who considered it a good lark; and what was remarkable was, that between eight and nine o'clock, the time at which the police change, was the time selected to play off these tricks". Plays and poems were written about him and racehorses named after him – *The Terror of London: Spring-heeled Jack* did the rounds of many provincial theatres in the 1860s and 1870s. By the last quarter of the nineteenth century, he was back in public imagination, increased sightings coinciding with greater notoriety thanks to the writers of thriller stories for the Penny Dreadfuls.

> *CAPTURE OF SPRING-HEELED JACK*
> *Yesterday James Painter, a youth about 18 years of age, and footman to Mrs Chater, of Kilburn, was charged at Marylebone police office … with having for some time past kept the fair inhabitants of the above village in considerable alarm, by sallying out upon them during their evening perambulations dressed as a ghost.*
>
> **Morning Post, 4 April 1838**

THE ITALIAN BOY MURDER

In the 1830s, London's medical schools were so desperate for corpses for use in anatomy classes that they were not often fussy about their origin. It was well known that so-called "resurrection men" robbed fresh graves for the fee offered by anatomists. In November 1831, however, when some men arrived at King's College Hospital carrying what seemed to be an unusually fresh corpse of a 14-year-old boy, the doctors were unable to turn a blind eye and called the police. The victim was identified as an Italian boy named Carlo Ferrier, and it soon became apparent that his was not the only suspicious death. The police headed to Nova Scotia Gardens, near Bethnal Green, whose tenants included resurrection men John Bishop, Thomas Williams and James May (a butcher). After a thorough investigation and trial, Bishop and Williams were found guilty of murder. They were hanged at Newgate Prison on 5 December 1831, in front of a massive crowd. As was usual practice for executed criminals, their corpses were passed to a medical school for anatomizing.

JACK THE RIPPER

In 1888, five women were brutally murdered in Whitechapel and a widespread terror began of a serial killer who purportedly wrote to Scotland Yard in victims' blood and whom the media named Jack the Ripper. The newspapers went crazy and women around the country were terrorized by the mere thought of walking alone. Prostitutes in the East End of London had no choice but to take their chances with each customer; the Ripper's five known victims were all very poor women working as prostitutes. The murderer's identity has never been proved. It is believed he (or she) did not kill again after November 1888, but there is no proof that the known victims were the only ones.

- Mary Ann Nicholls – murdered 31 August
- Annie Chapman – 8 September
- Elizabeth Stride and Catherine Eddowes – 30 September
- Mary Jane Kelly – 9 November
- A possible sixth victim was Martha Tabram, who was murdered on 6 August, but her killing was markedly different from the others.

POLISH IMMIGRANT, ARTIST OR QUEEN'S GRANDSON?

Many theories have been put forward as to the identity of Jack the Ripper and the mystery continues to fascinate people today.

- The police were convinced that the Ripper must have had medical knowledge, to have carried out the attacks so brutally and quickly. Others claim he might have been a butcher.
- In 1894, several London newspapers ran the story that a Metropolitan police officer had asserted the Ripper was a lunatic who had been incarcerated in Dartmoor Prison Asylum for another offence, hence had not killed since November 1888.
- In 1892, a report was published of a possible attempted murder by Jack the Ripper. *The Illustrated Police News* revealed the story of Emily Edith Smith, assaulted by a man who had lured her to Whitechapel. When she tried to get away, he took out a knife, but she fought him off by kneeing him in the groin and running. The police newspaper mentioned the similarity between the man she described and the one they had been seeking in connection with one of the Ripper murders.
- American author Patricia Cornwell wrote a book claiming the artist Walter Sickert was Jack the Ripper – but Sickert was in France with his family when four of the Ripper murders were committed.
- Prince Eddy, grandson of Queen Victoria, has long been suspected by Ripper fanatics.

- In 2014, it was claimed that new evidence had been found. DNA on a shawl from near one of the victims was said to have identified a Polish barber, Aaron Kosminski (*c.*1865–1919); the "discovery" was quickly discredited.

THE RILLINGTON PLACE MURDERS

- John Christie was a serial killer of at least six people, including his wife Ethel.
- Four of his victims were found beneath the floorboards at his home, 10 Rillington Place, in Notting Hill.
- He was executed at Pentonville Prison on 15 July 1953.
- 10 Rillington Place became such a notorious address and attracted so many ghoulish tourists that people campaigned for it to be demolished. The house was knocked down in the 1970s.

> *A neighbour told a reporter yesterday: "Mr and Mrs Christie were very quiet people who kept very much to themselves. Mr Christie said some weeks ago that his wife had gone to Birmingham to look after her sick father." … Late yesterday afternoon police officers in plain clothes arrived at the house in a car, accompanied by a civilian. They stayed there for about five minutes and when they came out the civilian, a middle-aged man, ducked his head to prevent the crowd from seeing him.*
> **Manchester Guardian, 26 March 1953**

POLICING LONDON

BOW STREET RUNNERS

In the 1740s, a new office with the purpose of regulating and maintaining law and order was opened at 4 Bow Street. The magistrate Henry Fielding joined the office (set up by Sir Thomas de Veil) and, together with his half-brother John Fielding (also a magistrate and social reformer), established what became known as the Bow Street Runners. These were the ancestors of the Metropolitan Police. Soon the City of London set up its own police force and another force was founded to patrol the river.

LONDON FACTS

Aged 19, John Fielding lost his sight, after an accident while in the Navy. Helped by his half-brother Henry, John set up in business and studied law. He became renowned as a pioneer of criminal justice, able to identify a person by their voice. His nickname was the "Blind Beak of Bow Street" (beak being slang for magistrate or judge).

METROPOLITAN POLICE FACTS

- In 1812–16, Robert Peel served as Chief Secretary for Ireland and founded an early police force, known as the Peace Preservation Force.
- In 1822, Peel was appointed Home Secretary and sought to reform the policing of London.
- In July 1829, an Act of Parliament created the Metropolitan Police; the first constables were seen on the streets of London in September 1830.
- The Metropolitan Police Act of 1829 defined the area in which the police had jurisdiction, taking Charing Cross as its centre and spanning out to a seven-mile radius. This did not include the City of London (which still maintains its own separate police force today).
- There were two Police commissioners when the force was founded: Richard Mayne (1796–1868) and Lieutenant-Colonel Sir Charles Rowan (*c.*1782–1852).
- The nicknames "Bobbies" and "Peelers" both come from Sir Robert Peel's name.
- The nickname "Old Bill" may refer to King William IV, who became king in 1830, shortly after the Metropolitan Police was founded.
- In 1830, the first policeman was killed on duty, patrolling in Euston.
- In one year, 1847, a total of 238 police officers were dismissed from the force for bad conduct, mostly drunkenness.
- The Great Exhibition of 1851 called for a new special police division.

SCOTLAND YARD

The original police headquarters was built on the site of the former Whitehall Palace, where the Scottish ambassador used to stay. In the 1960s, operations were moved to a new building near Victoria, known as New Scotland Yard.

THE CRIME MUSEUM

The Crime Museum or "Black Museum" located at New Scotland Yard details the history of crime and policing in London. It is open to researchers but not to the public. The collection includes weapons, crime-scene evidence and information about London's worst criminals, including Jack the Ripper. It is used by the Met for training and research.

POLICE MATRONS

In the 1890s, women finally began to feature in the Met. There was a call for female police workers in every station, to help protect women in custody. But until World War I, only a very few women were employed, as "police matrons"; instead, wives of police officers were often used for searches or examinations of female prisoners.

WOMEN IN THE MET FACTS

- In 1914, social campaigners Nina Boyle and Margaret Damer Dawson founded the Women Police Service (WPS). This was a separate body from the Metropolitan Police.
- In 1919, the Met acquired its first policewoman, Sofia Stanley. She helped design the first female police uniform, which became known as the Stanley Uniform.
- In 1923, female police officers were permitted to make arrests for the first time.
- Until 1946, policewomen had to give up their job if they married.
- In 1974, a new law forced the Met to pay women the same salaries as men.
- In 1995, the Met had its first female Chief Constable, Pauline Clare.
- The first female Assistant Commissioner of Scotland Yard was Cressida Dick, who took office in 2009.

THE FIRST DETECTIVES

Robert Peel's police force came in for a great deal of criticism, especially over its poor record in solving – rather than preventing – crimes. This changed after the creation of the Detective Department in 1842. The detectives were mainly concerned with the most serious crimes, particularly murder.

CHARLES DICKENS AND THE POLICE

Dickens's early writing about the police in *Oliver Twist* was an irreverent witty passage about the incompetent duo Blathers and Duff, but his first serious portrayal of detection was in *Martin Chuzzlewit*, in which he introduced Mr Nadgett, "a short, dried up, withered old man". Inspector Bucket in *Bleak House* was one of the first proper fictional detectives. His job allowed him to move with confidence in all areas of society and classes. Dickens described him as "Detective Mr Bucket with his forefinger, and his confidential manner impossible to be evaded or declined". Dickens was fascinated by the new London detectives. He went on patrol with them regularly, and became good friends with Inspector Charles Field, on whom he based Inspector Bucket.

PRISONS

London has had many prisons, some long destroyed. For centuries, Newgate was the most feared, as the site of public executions and an overcrowded, disease-ridden place. The oldest remaining prison is Brixton, opened in 1819 when Brixton was a village on the edge of the city. Until the nineteenth century, there were also debtors' prisons.

NEWGATE

This prison existed from the twelfth century until its demolition in 1902 (the Central Criminal Court, the Old Bailey, now stands on the site). Filthy and badly organized, it became synonymous with "gaol fever", nicknamed "Newgate fever". The illness was very contagious, and it was feared that anyone who visited or worked there could bring back the taint on their clothes and infect others. One of those to die of gaol fever within the prison was Lord George Gordon (of Gordon Riot fame), in prison for libel. In 1820, the *Morning Chronicle* reported:

> *The alarming increase of crime in the Metropolis, especially amongst the juvenile offenders, is to be chiefly attributed to the very inadequate state of Newgate Prison, for the purpose of classing the prisoners according to their various degrees of criminality; thus*

boys and girls, who may have been committed for some slight misdemeanours, are forced to associate with the basest and most hardened felons.

BRIXTON

- Brixton was the first London prison to use the treadmill as punishment. The power it generated ground flour to make prisoners' bread rations.
- The first governor of Brixton was a vicious, sadistic man named John Green who was sacked for drunkenness and violence.
- In the mid-nineteenth century, Brixton became a women's prison, with a female governor, Emma Martin, whose children grew up there.
- In the 1880s, Brixton had another reincarnation as a military prison.
- British Fascist leader Oswald Mosley was incarcerated there during World War II.
- Famous prisoners include Mick Jagger, Bertrand Russell, Terence MacSwiney and the Kray Twins.
- In the 1990s, Brixton had a reputation as one of the worst prisons in Britain, with stories of suicides, riots and bullying.
- In the 2010s, it was reinvented as a rehabilitation prison.

LONDON FACTS

In 2014, The Clink Restaurant opened inside Brixton Prison, training prisoners as chefs and restaurant staff. It was the idea of The Clink Charity and is open to the public. The website promises "a unique dining experience, within the walls of this Category C prison". It also offers private dining rooms and conference facilities.

BRIDEWELL

Built as a palace for Henry VIII, Bridewell features in Hans Holbein's painting *The Ambassadors* (1533). During the short reign of Henry's son, Edward VI, it was given to the public as an orphanage, hospital and "house of correction". The child inmates were educated and trained as apprentices. It was run jointly with the Bethlehem Hospital for the Insane ("Bedlam") and had its own doctor. In later years it became a prison.

PRISON CONDITIONS

Each sex has a workroom and a night-room. They lie in boxes, with a little straw, on the floor.... There are many excellent regulations in this establishment. The prisoners have a liberal allowance, suitable employment, and some proper instruction; but the visitor laments that they are not more separated ... no other prison in London has any straw or bedding....

Prison reformer John Howard, *An Account of the Principal Lazarettos in Europe,* **1789**

PENTONVILLE

Opened in 1842, Pentonville was one of several prisons designed on principles espoused by the philosopher Jeremy Bentham. It was a "Panopticon", with cells spanning out from a central building from which guards could keep watch. There were cells for sole occupation – a design later criticized as enforcing solitary confinement. When it was built, however, Pentonville was hailed as a model prison. On 28 April 1845, the *Morning Post* published a glowing article: "There is in each cell a gas-light and water-closet, with washing-basin, and means of affording a daily supply of six gallons of water; and bell and label, by which a prisoner, whenever it is needful, can communicate with an officer of the prison; and all necessary furniture and fittings." In 1902, Pentonville became the gaol for prisoners condemned to death. It was also where public executioners were trained. Among those hanged here was Dr Hawley Harvey Crippen, in 1910. It is still a working prison.

HOLLOWAY

Built in 1849–52, as the City of London House of Correction, Holloway housed male, female and child prisoners. One of its most famous was Oscar Wilde, incarcerated there in 1895 while awaiting trial for "gross indecency". Once convicted, he was imprisoned outside London, in Reading. In 1903, Holloway became a women-only prison and held female executions; two women were hanged together for "baby farming" and murdering babies in their charge. In 1906, the first suffragette prisoners were sent to Holloway and the prison gained notoriety for force-feeding, physical punishment and other abuses. Holloway saw the execution of Ruth Ellis in 1955 for the murder of her lover – the last woman to be hanged in Britain. In the 1970s, it was rebuilt, and now includes cells for mothers with babies.

WORMWOOD SCRUBS

"The Scrubs" is a men's prison in west London, north of White City. It was designed by Edmond Du Cane, after whom Du Cane Road, where it stands, is named, and was built by prisoner labourers in 1875–91. During World War II, part of the prison was given over to war administration. Wormwood Scrubs's distinctive, forbidding Victorian façade has made it a popular filming location, appearing on numerous TV shows as well as in the Michael Caine film *The Italian Job*.

DEBTORS' PRISONS

The principal debtors' prisons in London were the Fleet, Marshalsea, King's Bench, Queen's Bench and Whitecross Street.

- The first Fleet Prison was built in the twelfth century, on the banks of the River Fleet. It was rebuilt several times. Famous inmates included the poet John Donne, imprisoned for marrying without obtaining consent from his new wife's father. The prison became infamous for so-called "Fleet marriages": secret weddings performed in the prison chapel by debtor clergymen incarcerated there. The prevalence of Fleet marriages – without parental consent or a licence – led to the Marriage Act of 1753.
- The King's Bench Prison, rebuilt in the 1750s in an area of Southwark known as St George's Fields, was where aristocratic debtors were usually sent; families and friends were expected to pay higher-than-usual sums for their food and rent. The other inmates lived in squalor, at a prison frequently berated in the press for filthy, overcrowded conditions. In 1768, radical MP and journalist John Wilkes was imprisoned here for criticizing George III. When several thousand people gathered in his support, the military opened fire and killed several – leading to riots all over London.
- In 1824, John Dickens, a payroll clerk with the Navy, was sent to the Marshalsea. In time his wife Elizabeth and their younger children joined him, which was usual practice. Their eldest son, Charles, was 12 years old. He lived alone in a lodging house and worked in a factory to pay

for his whole family's food and accommodation in the prison. In 1855–57 he published in instalments his novel *Little Dorrit*, whose central character, Amy Dorrit, is born inside the Marshalsea, where her father is imprisoned for debt. Today, all that remains is a wall bordering the graveyard of St George's Church in Southwark. The wall has a Blue Plaque to John Dickens.

> *Thirty years ago there stood, a few doors short of the church of Saint George, in the borough of Southwark, on the left-hand side of the way going southward, the Marshalsea Prison. It had stood there many years before, and it remained there some years afterwards; but it is gone now, and the world is none the worse without it. It was an oblong pile of barrack building, partitioned into squalid houses standing back to back, so that there were no back rooms; environed by a narrow paved yard, hemmed in by high walls duly spiked at top.*
>
> **Charles Dickens, *Little Dorrit*, 1857**

FAMOUS LONDONERS

Octavia Hill (1838–1912) grew up in Cambridgeshire with a father continually in and out of debt: Octavia saw how easily people could end up in poverty. When the family moved to London, her first job was as manager and bookkeeper of the Ladies' Cooperative Guild in Russell Square. She and her mother also volunteered at a ragged school. Through her work and her social group, she made influential friendships with wealthy philanthropists, including John Ruskin and F.D. Maurice. She was adept at identifying where charitable projects were needed and persuading moneyed friends to finance her ideas, most notably the Octavia Housing Trust. She is best remembered as one of the founders of the National Trust.

8

CIVIL RIGHTS, PROTEST AND RIOTS

As capital city and home to the government and the monarch, London has often been a focus for public fury. Trafalgar Square in particular has witnessed many a scene of political demonstration and civil unrest.

THE PEASANTS' REVOLT

In the late twelfth century people all over Britain were arguing about a new levy: the Poll Tax. The government had embroiled Britain in a war with France and needed money to pay for it, but the people, most of whom could barely earn enough to feed their families, had had enough. On 30 May 1381, a tax collector in Essex tried to force people to pay, and the spark that became the Peasants' Revolt was ignited. Soon the revolution had spread from Essex to Norfolk and the rebels marched on London. There, they attacked politicians' houses and demanded to meet the King. On 15 June, 14-year-old Richard II met the rebel leader, Wat Tyler, at Mile End and agreed to parts of his demands; some of the mob dispersed, but others, including Tyler, stayed on and continued to wreak havoc. The King met Tyler again, at Smithfield, where several of the King's men, including William Walworth, Mayor of London, were so angered by what they saw as Tyler's lack of respect that he was dragged from his horse and killed. After the mob had gone, the King's troops travelled around the country killing anyone they suspected of taking part in the revolt. The Peasants' Revolt ended in the deaths of many rebels – but it also ended the hated Poll Tax.

LONDON AND SLAVERY

- In the reign of Elizabeth I, merchant John Hawkins raised funding for a trip to Africa. Despite having given his queen assurance that no one would be enslaved without their permission, Hawkins went to Sierra Leone and took around 300 people by violence, forcing them to become slaves. He sold them to plantation owners in the West Indies.
- The Royal African Company was granted a monopoly over slave trading on the west coast of Africa. Its headquarters was in Leadenhall Street.
- The East India Company was founded in 1600. In addition to trading in spices and textiles, it ran a lucrative trade in transporting slaves via Madagascar.
- The Royal Adventurers into Africa was granted a royal charter by Charles II in 1660.
- The Jamaica Coffee House in St Michael's Alley was where slave traders would meet and discuss business.
- Sir William Beckford, owner of slave plantations in Jamaica, was Lord Mayor of London twice. There is a statue of Beckford at the Guildhall.
- Liverpool, Bristol and London dominated the British slave trade.
- The West India Docks welcomed slaving ships from the Caribbean.
- Two of the earliest British campaigners against the trade were brothers Granville and William Sharp, who befriended a slave named Jonathan Strong in the 1760s. William, a doctor, treated the injured slave after finding him on the street; when they heard his story, Granville used his legal knowledge to fight Jonathan's case – he was successful and soon began defending other slaves.
- From the 1780s onwards the anti-slavery movement grew. Abolitionists Thomas Clarkson and William Wilberforce, along with potter Josiah Wedgwood, publicized the campaign, so that the true horrors of slavery were talked about and abhorred.

FAMOUS LONDONERS

Ignatius Sancho (1729–80) was born on a slave ship headed for Grenada. The conditions were so brutal that his mother died and his father killed himself before Ignatius was two years old. The orphaned child was brought to London, where he worked as a servant and ended up in the household of the Duke of Montagu. There he became a prodigious musician and, as an adult, a fervent anti-slavery campaigner. He and his wife set up a grocery shop in central London, which became a fashionable meeting place for musicians, writers and thinkers. Renowned as a composer and playwright, Sancho was also the first "black person of African origin" permitted to vote.

One day, when all our people were gone out to their works as usual, and only I and my dear sister were left to mind the house, two men and a woman got over our walls, and in a moment seized us both. My sister and I were separated and I ended up in the hands of a slave dealer who supplied the Atlantic slave ships. Six months later I found myself on board a slave ship.

Extract from *The Interesting Narrative of the Life of Olaudah Equiano*, 1789

FAMOUS LONDONERS

Olaudah Equiano (*c.*1747–97) was kidnapped as a child from Africa (present-day Nigeria) and sold into slavery, first in Barbados and then Virginia. In the 1750s he was bought by an English naval captain, Captain Pascal, for whom he worked on-board ship and then in Blackheath, where he was given a rudimentary education. He was later sold twice, but also made some money from working, and eventually bought his freedom. He worked as a paid sailor before ending up in London, where he made contact with abolitionists including Granville Sharp. He travelled and attempted to ease the conditions of enslaved workers on plantations, with limited success, so he returned to London and fought slavery by legal means. He formed the group Sons of Africa and supported anti-slavery campaigners. In 1789, he published his best-selling autobiography: *The Interesting Narrative of the Life of Olaudah Equiano*. Three years later he married Susan Cullen, who assisted him in travelling around the country to speak about slavery. He died in 1797, aged around 50.

THE GORDON RIOTS

In 1780, the anti-Catholic agitator Lord George Gordon (1751–93) called for a return to the bad old days of religious intolerance. Two years previously, the Catholic Relief Act had been passed, sweeping away years of oppression and legally sanctioned abuse against Catholics in Protestant-dominated England. Gordon was one of the leading figures in the "no popery" anti-Catholic movement, and on 2 June 1780 he marched with an angry mob of 60,000 protestors to the House of Commons. The anti-Catholic feeling incited led to days of violence and rioting throughout London, even reaching into Newgate Prison, whose buildings were attacked and prisoners helped to freedom. The army was called in to suppress the rebellion. Many rioters were arrested and punished, and Gordon was tried for treason. He was acquitted.

SUNDAY TRADING RIOTS

An estimated 150,000 people demonstrated in Hyde Park in 1855 to protest against a Sunday Trading Bill aimed at restricting trade on Sundays. As Sunday was the only free day for most working people, there was great resistance to this law, proposed in the name of Christianity. Stories of the riot and the violence meted out to demonstrators by the police made headline news all over the country. On 9 January 1856, the *Hereford Journal* reported on the trial at the Old Bailey "of the police constable against whom indictments were preferred ... for violently assaulting several persons".

BLACK MONDAY, 1886

The London United Workmen's Committee and the Social Democratic Federation both held a demonstration about unemployment in Trafalgar Square on 8 February 1886. Afterwards, fights broke out between the two organizations and the crowd became a riotous mob. Most of the police hastened to stand guard around Buckingham Palace, leaving the crowd unchecked. Wealthy householders on Pall Mall, in St James's and around Hyde Park had their windows smashed and stones thrown against their walls and doors. The following day, the *London Standard* reported,

"The workmen's demonstration passed off quietly enough, but the 'Social Democrats', at the close of their meeting, proceeded to the commission of a series of dreadful outrages, the like of which have not been known in London for many years," and told of looting of shops on St James's Street.

BLOODY SUNDAY, 1887

On 13 November 1887, Socialist groups were marching to Trafalgar Square to demonstrate in favour of free speech and against repression in Ireland, when police and soldiers weighed in violently to break up what had been a peaceful demonstration. Three people were killed as mounted police charged at the mob. The day became known as "Bloody Sunday". A week later, on 20 November, another protest march headed to Trafalgar Square, this time to protest about the police brutality. One person was killed: his name was Alfred Linnell, and he was unaware of the march and its causes, having been merely caught up in it on his way home from work. There was public outcry, one of the most celebrated voices belonging to designer and writer William Morris. Linnell was perceived as a martyr, and given a public funeral. William Morris wrote a poem, "Death Song for Alfred Linnell", which was put to music and sung at the funeral.

BLACK FRIDAY, 1910

On 18 November 1910, women's suffrage leaders Elizabeth Garrett Anderson and Emmeline Pankhurst led a protest march to the House of Commons to petition Prime Minister Herbert Asquith. The march started at Caxton Hall in Westminster, and was attended by relatively militant suffragettes from the WSPU (Women's Social and Political Union) and less radical suffragists from the NUWSS (National Union of Women's Suffrage Societies) as well as male supporters. The Prime Minister had no intention of meeting the women, and the police permitted an angry, yelling mob to assault the marchers both verbally and physically; the police also joined in. A report into the events of Black Friday claimed that Asquith and his Home Secretary Winston Churchill suggested that the police use sexual violence against the suffrage campaigners and that many members of the unruly mob were police officers out of uniform. *Votes for Women* of 25 November 1910 reported: "The orders of the Home Secretary were, apparently, that the police were to be present both in uniform and also in plain clothes among the crowd and that the women were to be thrown from one to the other." Around 150 suffragettes were hurt in the violence and several later died as a result of injuries sustained that day.

FAMOUS LONDONERS

Elizabeth Garrett (1836–1917), daughter of a pawnbroker, grew up in east London. Her parents were unusual in that they insisted all their daughters had as good an education as boys; Elizabeth proved to have an exceptional academic brain. When Dr Elizabeth Blackwell, the first female doctor in the United States, came to London, Elizabeth Garrett met her and was inspired. She was refused entry to medical school on account of her gender, so enrolled as a nurse and attended medical students' classes; but the male students complained and she was banned. Persisting, in 1865 she passed the Society of Apothecaries' exam, obtaining the relevant qualifications to be a doctor. She was still not permitted – and the loophole that had allowed her to sit the exam was plugged. Elizabeth then attained a medical degree in Paris, but was still not allowed to register in England. Meantime, she married James Anderson. In 1872, she founded The New Hospital for Women, now the Elizabeth Garrett Anderson Hospital, and continued to campaign for women's rights and her own right to be recognized by the medical profession. In 1876, the law was changed to permit women to become doctors.

NOTTING HILL RACE RIOT 1958

In the summer of 1958, riots broke out in Notting Hill. For months, gangs of white men had been harassing black families who had recently moved to the area. The gangs were encouraged by the briefly resurgent Fascist leader Oswald Mosley, who held meetings in the area, using the slogan "Keep Britain White". Caribbean businesses and restaurants had been attacked and five incidents of racist assault were carried out against black men. On the night of 30 August a protest riot exploded onto the streets; it gathered force and lasted until 5 September.

VIETNAM WAR PROTEST

- Around 4,000 people took part in an anti-Vietnam War rally outside the American Embassy in Grosvenor Square in July 1966: 31 were arrested.
- In March 1968, an estimated 10,000 people rallied in Trafalgar Square to protest against the Vietnam War. Actress Vanessa Redgrave was one of the speakers. When a procession marched to the American Embassy, the rally turned violent. The BBC reported that more than 200 people were arrested and 50 were taken to hospital.

BRIXTON RIOTS

- In April 1981, three days of rioting broke out in Brixton, at the time a very poor and rundown area, following rumours of a racist incident of police brutality. It was claimed that around 5,000 people took part in the riots and 300 were injured. Afterwards the media accused the Metropolitan Police of "institutional racism", but a report by Lord Scarman denied this – although he made recommendations for more egalitarian policing. However, 18 years after Scarman's results were published, a report into the 1993 murder of Stephen Lawrence came up with the opposite result, claiming racism was rife in London policing.
- In 1985, race riots broke out in Brixton again, after the shooting of a black woman in her home by white police officers. Dorothy "Cherry" Groce was paralysed from the chest down after being shot when police raided her house, looking for her son. On 30 September, *The Guardian* reported: "Major crimes discovered totalled 137, 58 of them burglaries, and 55 motor vehicles had been burnt or damaged in the rioting which erupted after petrol bombs had been thrown at Brixton police station on Saturday night. Forty-three civilians and 10 police officers were hurt."

THE POLL TAX RIOTS

In 1990, riots broke out across Britain against the government's plans for a new Poll Tax. This tax was to be levied against everyone regardless of earnings. Everyone was to be taxed the same – and it was this that ignited the sparks of rebellion. On 31 March, a huge protest began in London and turned into what became dubbed by the media "the Poll Tax riots".

Around 100,000 people took to the streets of London, and what began as a peaceful protest soon erupted into fury and violent clashes between police and crowds. The BBC reported, "London has erupted into the worst riots seen in the city for a century," and shared eyewitness comments about "a cloud of black smoke over Trafalgar Square". The Poll Tax (which did not become law) was considered to have led directly to Prime Minister Margaret Thatcher's political downfall.

MARCHING AGAINST THE IRAQ WAR

In February 2003, the UK's biggest-ever demonstration took place. Police reported that 750,000 people attended, but the march's organizers gave figures of over two million. The demonstration, timed to happen at the same time as others all over the country, was in protest at the war in Iraq. The only arrests were for minor offences, such as four people who staged a sit-in in the middle of the road, closing off Piccadilly Circus to traffic.

THE RIOTS OF 2011

On 4 August 2011, a man named Mark Duggan was shot dead by police in Tottenham. Peaceful protest began almost immediately, but on 6 August it turned to rioting in Tottenham. Over the next few days, riots spread across London – and to other British cities. They did not entirely subside until 12 August. Throughout London, banks, businesses and shops were attacked, looted and set on fire, and homes above targeted buildings were also destroyed. In Ealing, 68-year-old Richard Mannington Bowes was attacked and killed by a 17-year-old as he tried to put out a fire started by rioters. Over 1,800 people were arrested in London alone and over 1,000 were charged with criminal offences; the youngest rioter arrested was 11 years old, and around half of those taken to court were under 21. In addition to the shooting of Mark Duggan, the causes of the riots were variously claimed to be a scandal over MPs' expenses, the recession and austerity measures, and a lack of trust in the police and government. Londoners living through the riots and the newspapers were united in their anger about the lack of police on the streets during the riots – which was blamed on recent government cuts to police numbers. *The Guardian* newspaper estimated the "minimum cost of the riots" to be £100 million.

9

PLAGUE AND FIRE

In September 1348, London was hit by a terrible disease, the Bubonic Plague, believed to have been brought on a ship from continental Europe. Although it could never be proved, it was suspected that the plague-carrying cargo was on a wool ship. Within a year of the Bubonic Plague's arrival in London, it was estimated to have killed around half of all Londoners.

In 1665, the Great Plague hit London. Many people fled from their homes, hoping that if they were in the fresh air, they might avoid catching the plague. Open spaces, such as Hyde Park, became places of refuge. The Great Plague was believed to have been brought to an end by another catastrophe, the Great Fire of London in 1666, which swept away disease as it razed much of the city to the ground.

FAMOUS LONDONERS

Samuel Pepys (1633–1703) worked for Edward Montagu, a military commander for the Puritans who ended up switching sides to the Royalists. Pepys is famous today because of his minutely detailed diary, which chronicles London life through the 1660s. It gives an everyday insight into the Restoration of the monarchy, the Great Plague and the Great Fire, as well as minutiae of life and social behaviour.

Diary extract 10 June 1665:
In the evening home to supper, and there to my great trouble hear that the plague is come into the City (though it hath these three or four weeks since its beginning been wholly out of the

City); but where should it begin but in my good friend and
neighbour's, Dr Burnett in Fanchurch-street – which in both
points troubles me mightily. To the office to finish my letters, and
then home to bed – being troubled at the sickness, and my head
filled also with other business enough, and perticularly how to
put my things and estate in order, in case it should please God to
call me away – which God dispose of to his own glory.

GREAT FIRE OF LONDON

In 1666, Londoners sweltered under a long, hot and very dry summer. By
the end of August, the wood of which so many buildings were constructed
was as dry as kindling. So when, early in the morning on 2 September,
a fire broke out, it was to have disastrous results. It began in Thomas
Farriner's baker's shop, in the appropriately named Pudding Lane, not far
from St Paul's Cathedral. The fire was believed to have started at around
1 a.m., possibly caused by a spark falling out of Farriner's oven and on to
a pile of fuel. It was fanned by a strong easterly wind, which played the
flames out of the bakery and on to nearby buildings. As London was so
very crowded and buildings so close together that, in some places, streets
were too narrow for a laden horse to pass through, there was plenty of fuel
to keep the fire raging.

Londoners fled as fast as they could. Farriner and his family climbed
over rooftops and escaped down to the street via a neighbour's house – but
the fire's first victim was their maid. Those who lived closest to Pudding
Lane could not take many possessions, as it was all happening much too
rapidly; most had time simply to grab their children and anything portable
to hand, and run. Those who lived slightly further away boxed up
whatever they could and left their homes quickly. Initially, the seriousness
of the fire was scorned by those in power, with the Mayor of London, Sir
Thomas Bloodworth, famously remarking "a woman might piss it out".
He was proved embarrassingly wrong: over 13,000 homes and businesses
were destroyed, as well as civic buildings, dozens of churches and St Paul's
Cathedral. Of those who stayed to fight the fire, most notable were King
Charles II and his brother James, Duke of York. When it became clear that
the fire was not under control, the King sent his guards, ordering them to
pull down houses in order to stop the fire in its tracks. The Duke and the

King also took an active role in fighting the fire, initially by giving orders to others but when the fire continued to rage into a second day the King was seen wading through the water that by now filled the streets, hurling water from a bucket onto the flames and armed with tools to help bring down houses. Many Londoners had fled to open spaces, most gathering at Moorfields. So the King went to address them, and ordered food and drink to be sent there and distributed.

LONDON FACTS

A gilt-covered cherub on the corner of Cock Lane and Giltspur Street in the City of London marks the place where the last embers of the fire were reputed to have burnt themselves out. It is known as Pie Corner.

After the fire was finally extinguished, the public looked for someone to blame. A papist plot was suspected and, instead of blaming nature or an accident, the finger of suspicion was raised against a "foreigner": a Frenchman, Robert Hubert, who was arrested in Romford, Essex, several days after the fire. Despite the facts that Hubert was not a Catholic, and – more importantly – had not been in England when the fire started, for some reason he confessed to the crime, claiming that he was part of a large terrorist organization, run from Paris. Even at the time, the prosecutors had their doubts – not least because his confession included graphic descriptions of pushing incendiary devices through a window, and yet Farriner himself protested that such a window never existed. The case went to trial. The jury believed Hubert was insane and had made up his story, and the Lord Chief Justice said he did not believe the Frenchman was guilty – but the government needed a scapegoat so Hubert was duly found guilty. He was hanged at Tyburn on 27 October 1666. The watching crowd reportedly turned into an angry mob, believing Hubert had destroyed their city, and after his body was taken down from the scaffold it was alleged to have been torn to pieces. Just days later, it was discovered, irrefutably, that on the date of the fire Hubert had been on board the ship that would take him to London. The fire was eventually ruled an accident.

Methinks already from this chymic flame
I see a city of more precious mould,
Rich as the town which gives the Indies name,
With silver paved and all divine with gold.

Already, labouring with a mighty fate,
She shakes the rubbish from her mounting brow,
And seems to have renewed her charter's date,
Which Heaven will to the death of time allow.

More great than human now and more August,
New deified she from her fires does rise:
Hew widening streets on new foundations trust,
And, opening, into larger parts she flies.

John Dryden, "London after the Great Fire, 1666"

THE MONUMENT

King Charles II appointed six commissioners to help rebuild London, with
Christopher Wren as principal architect. Wren also oversaw the design of
a monument to those who had died in the Great Fire. Official figures of
the dead were astoundingly low – fewer than 10 – but it is likely that many
poor people, particularly those from illiterate families who did not know
how to register a death, were uncounted and their deaths unrecorded. The
Monument stands at the site of Thomas Farriner's bakery and has given
a new name to the street, Monument Street. The Monument, designed by
Robert Hooke, is in the style of an antique Doric column.

10

RELIGIOUS BUILDINGS

ST PAUL'S CATHEDRAL

The first cathedral in London, dedicated to St Paul, was built in AD 604. It was subject to regular attacks by Vikings and was frequently damaged by fires and battles. In the 1080s, during the reign of William the Conqueror, a new and more enduring St Paul's Cathedral was built, overseen by Bishop Maurice, the King's chaplain. This building survived for almost 600 years.

In June 1561, the cathedral was struck by lightning. Architect Inigo Jones was commissioned to restore the damaged building, but the outbreak of the Civil War in 1642 meant his project was never finished. Oliver Cromwell's forces took over the cathedral and used it as a stable for their horses and barracks for their troops. After the Restoration of the monarchy in 1660, when Charles II came to the throne, Christopher Wren was invited to put forward plans for reconstruction, and he suggested adding an impressive dome. In the end, Wren had to design an entirely new cathedral, following the Great Fire of London in 1666.

When Wren and his workmen were sorting through the rubble of the old cathedral, they happened upon part of an old gravestone, carved with the single word resurgam ("I shall rise again"). Wren saw this as prophetic and used the stone as his centrepiece for the Cathedral's south transept, placing it below a carving of a phoenix rising from the ashes. When Wren died, he was buried in St Paul's. His grave bears an inscription in Latin which, when translated, means: "If you would see his monument, look around."

◇◇

THE DOME

The dome of St Paul's is 34 m (111 ft) high and weighs 65,000 tonnes. The lowest of its three galleries is the Whispering Gallery, more than 30 m (98 ft) above the cathedral floor. Visitors can reach it by climbing 257 steps, and test its acoustics – it takes its name from the fact that if two people stand on opposite sides of the dome, one can whisper against the walls and be heard on the other side.

◇◇

CHRISTOPHER WREN'S CHURCHES IN LONDON

- St Benet, Paul's Wharf (1677–83)
- St Clement, Eastcheap (1683–87)
- St Edmund, King and Martyr, Lombard Street (1670–79)
- St James, Garlickhythe (1676–83)
- St Margaret Pattens, Eastcheap (1684–87)
- St Martin, Ludgate (1677–84)
- St Mary, Abchurch (1681–86)
- St Mary, Aldermary (1679–82)
- St Michael, Cornhill (1669–72)
- St Paul's Cathedral (1675–1711)
- St Peter upon Cornhill (1677–84)
- St Stephen, Walbrook (1672–79)
- St Magnus-the-Martyr, Lower Thames Street (1671–87)
- St Mary-at-Hill, Lovat Lane (1670–76)

WREN CHURCHES DAMAGED IN
THE BLITZ BUT REBUILT TO HIS DESIGNS

- St Andrew-by-the-Wardrobe, Queen Victoria Street (1685–95)
- St Andrew, Holborn (1686–87)
- St Anne and St Agnes, Gresham Street (1676–87)
- St Bride's Church, Fleet Street (1670–84)
- St Lawrence Jewry, Gresham Street (1670–86)
- St Mary-le-Bow, Cheapside (1670–83)
- St Michael Paternoster Royal, College Hill (1686–94)
- St Nicholas Cole Abbey, Queen Victoria Street (1671–81)
- St Vedast, Foster Lane (1670–97)

WESTMINSTER ABBEY

In the tenth century, Benedictine monks established their home on the site of present-day Westminster Abbey, and in 1042 King Edward the Confessor ordered a new church to be built here, but died before he could enjoy it. The first coronation performed at the abbey was on Christmas Day in 1066, of William the Conqueror, and every successive monarch has been crowned here. The church that William knew is no longer standing, as the current abbey dates back to 1245 and the reign of Henry III. Over 3,000 people are buried at Westminster Abbey, including 17 monarchs.

FAMOUS NAMES IN WESTMINSTER ABBEY

Some of these people are buried in the abbey itself; others are buried elsewhere, with a memorial in the abbey.

- Robert Adam
- Matthew Arnold
- Dame Peggy Ashcroft
- Clement Attlee
- W.H. Auden
- Jane Austen
- Lord and Lady Baden-Powell
- Stanley Baldwin
- Aphra Benn
- Robert Browning
- Geoffrey Chaucer
- Oliver Cromwell
- Charles Darwin
- Charles Dickens
- John Dryden
- George Eliot
- David Garrick
- William Ewart Gladstone
- George Frideric Handel
- Thomas Hardy
- Samuel Johnson
- Ben Jonson

- David Livingstone
- John Masefield
- Sir Isaac Newton
- Sir Laurence Olivier
- William Pitt, the Younger
- Henry Purcell
- Alfred, Lord Tennyson
- William Wilberforce
- Oscar Wilde

WESTMINSTER ABBEY FACTS

- Despite being a Puritan and therefore a "dissenter", Oliver Cromwell was given a state funeral at Westminster Abbey and buried there. After the Restoration of the monarchy, his body was disinterred and taken to the execution site at Tyburn. There his two-year-old corpse was hanged from the Tyburn tree, then taken down and decapitated. His final burial place was kept secret from the public, but was very close to present-day Marble Arch.
- The Poet Laureate Ben Jonson, who died in 1637, was buried standing upright.
- The abbey has its own museum. Among its artefacts are wax effigies of centuries of English monarchs.
- The abbey's garden was originally a medicinal garden kept by the monks.
- The tomb of Lady Elizabeth Nightingale has the horrifying sculpture of a skeleton emerging from her tomb.
- The abbey's first royal wedding, of King Henry I and Queen Matilda, took place in 1100.
- Every year, on 9 June, the anniversary of Charles Dickens's death, a wreath-laying ceremony is held at his grave in Poets' Corner, by members of the Dickens Fellowship and Dickens family.

Poets' Corner, one of the most famous parts of the abbey, grew up around Geoffrey Chaucer's and Edmund Spencer's graves in the south transept. Not all the poets and authors honoured here are buried here – some of the most famous, including William Shakespeare, Byron, George Eliot and Oscar Wilde, are only memorialized. Byron, Eliot and Wilde were all considered too scandalous to have any memorial here until the late twentieth century. Oscar Wilde's memorial, a stained-glass window, was not granted until 1995, almost a century after his death.

FAMOUS LONDONERS

Geoffrey Chaucer was born in London in *c*.1340 to a prosperous wine merchant and his wife. In his teens the young poet was employed by Countess Elizabeth of Ulster, through whom he had access to the royal court, and went to France as a soldier in what has become known as The Hundred Years' War. He was captured and became a prisoner of war; his royal connections saved him and the required ransom was paid. His most famous work is *The Canterbury Tales*, which he had not completed when he died. After his death in 1400, he was buried in Westminster Abbey, in the area later known as Poets' Corner.

ALL HALLOWS BY THE TOWER

The oldest church in the City of London dates back to AD 675. In 1926, building work uncovered a second-century Roman pavement beneath it. The church has significant historic associations with US history: William Penn was baptised here and John Quincy Adams was married.

TEMPLE CHURCH

This is the only round church in London, and one of just four left in England (the other three are in Cambridge, Essex and Northampton). It was built by the Knights Templar during the twelfth-century Crusades and was consecrated in 1185.

ST PAUL'S, COVENT GARDEN

Built by Inigo Jones in 1633, "The Actors' Church" owes its long association with the thespian profession to its location close to theatreland; it is an active church, but also a performance space, with plays regularly performed around its grounds. There are memorials to many famous theatrical people, including Noël Coward, Gracie Fields, Edith Evans, Vivien Leigh, Ivor Novello, Charlie Chaplin and Ellen Terry. Look closely at Ellen Terry's memorial to see where her birth date was changed – after her death it was discovered that the year she had believed she was born, 1848, was incorrect. Her birth certificate shows she was born in 1847; her father had lied about her age to make her childhood theatrical debut more impressive.

WESTMINSTER CATHEDRAL

This is London's Catholic cathedral. Its foundation stone was laid in 1895 and the cathedral was completed in 1903 to designs by architect John Francis Bentley. The now-controversial sculptor Eric Gill carved the 14 Stations of the Cross.

ST JAMES'S, SPANISH PLACE

One of the largest churches in London, this was one of the first Catholic churches permitted when British Catholics were still persecuted for their religion in the late eighteenth century. It was permissible because it was next to the Spanish ambassador's residence, Hertford House (now the Wallace Collection), as the ambassador's personal chapel.

ST PANCRAS CHURCH

Built in 1819, the church cost almost £90,000, a fortune at that date. It followed neoclassical style – the fervour for archaeology was at its height – complete with caryatids holding up the roof.

THE GREAT MOSQUE

The building now known as the Jamme Masjid, or Great Mosque, in Spitalfields was originally built in 1742 as a church, called the Neuve Eglise, for French Huguenots. In the early nineteenth century it became the place of worship for an evangelical Christian group named the Society for Propagating Christianity among the Jews. This was a short-lived project and the building became a Methodist chapel in 1819. By the end of the century, Spitalfields had become a predominantly Jewish area and it was turned into the Great Synagogue. It then became a mosque in the 1970s, when the population was largely Bangladeshi. The building is Grade II listed, and the original sundial, placed there by the Huguenots, can still be seen above the entrance, with its motto *umbra sumus* or "we are shadow".

LONDON CENTRAL MOSQUE

Regent's Park's mosque is also home to the Islamic Cultural Centre. In the 1940s the British government recognized the need for a mosque to serve London's Muslim community. Winston Churchill's administration gave £100,000 to buy a site. A 1-ha (2.3-acre) site near Hanover Gate was chosen and was opened in 1944 by King George VI, but it took over two decades before building work began. After a competition in 1969, architect Frederick Gibberd was chosen; construction work began in 1974 and continued until 1977. The mosque cost £6.5 million to build.

BEVIS MARKS SYNAGOGUE

The oldest synagogue in Britain was opened in 1701 in a quiet courtyard off one of the largest roads in the City of London – it had to be sited away from the main road because at that time Jews were not allowed to build on public thoroughfares. The synagogue is now surrounded by expensive offices, but originally it had its own school, orphanage and almshouse for the Jewish community. Legend has it that Queen Anne gave an oak beam from one of her Navy's ships to be used in building the ceiling. In the 1990s, the synagogue was damaged twice by IRA bombs, and rebuilt.

CENTRAL SYNAGOGUE

Located on or around Great Portland Street since 1870, the synagogue had its foundation stone laid by Baron Lionel de Rothschild in 1868. The original building was destroyed by German bombs in 1941. In 1946, a temporary synagogue was created and designs begun for a new building. It was rebuilt in 1958. In 2008, a Golden Jubilee service was held to commemorate 50 years of the new synagogue.

NEASDEN TEMPLE

London's first traditional Hindu temple, the Mandir, was built in Neasden using 5,000 tonnes of marble from India and Italy as well as limestone from Bulgaria. The entire building was carved in India before the pieces were transported to London and assembled on site. Building work began in 1992 and was completed in 1995. It was the first traditional Hindu stone temple in Europe. As well as the temple, the complex comprises a cultural centre, gym, bookshop, exhibition centre and administration offices.

HUGUENOTS

In the 1670s, London saw a major influx of French refugees from religious persecution. Most were Huguenots, Protestants no longer tolerated in Catholic France – under King Louis XIV, Protestantism was banned. Tens of thousands of Huguenots came, many of them weavers; the majority settled in London, creating a French community around Spitalfields. In 1687 a Huguenot burial ground, Mount Nod, was established in Wandsworth, and in 1718 a French Hospital, La Providence, was founded in Finsbury.

> *'Twas August, and the fierce sun overhead*
> *Smote on the squalid streets of Bethnal Green,*
> *And the pale weaver, through his windows seen*
> *In Spitalfields, looked thrice dispirited.*
>
> **Matthew Arnold, "East London", 1867**

THE TEMPLE OF MITHRAS

In 1954, while preparing for an office block, archaeologists uncovered the remains of an ancient temple, dedicated to Mithras, god of light. His cult originated in Persia and became popular among Roman soldiers, who probably brought it to Britain. The discovery drew thousands of people to Walbrook in the City. On a single day, an estimated 35,000 people came to view the temple. In the 1960s, it was carefully reconstructed about 100 m (330 ft) from its original site. In 2011, it was removed for more building work, and preparations made to rebuild it on its original site, in a purpose-built space beneath Bloomberg's European Headquarters.

11

THE RIVER THAMES AND OTHER WATERS

The Thames is the reason that the Celts, Romans and Anglo-Saxons all fought to establish their settlement in what is now London, on what had been agricultural land. In ancient times, the river was perceived to be a sacred body of water, into which ceremonial offerings were thrown. For centuries, it was the main thoroughfare of London, clogged with working boats. The earliest known written reference to the river by name was recorded by Julius Caesar in 54 BC:

I led the army to the River Thames and the territory of Cassivellaunus. There is only one place where the river can be forded, and even there with difficulty. When we reached it, I noticed large enemy forces drawn up on the opposite bank. The bank had also been fortified with sharp stakes fixed along it, and, as I discovered from prisoners and deserters, similar stakes had been driven into the river bed and were concealed beneath the water.

HISTORIC FLOODS

There was last night the greatest tide that ever was remembered in England to have been in this River, all Whitehall having been drowned.

Samuel Pepys, diary entry, 7 December 1663

LONDON BRIDGE

The original London Bridge, begun in 1176 and completed in 1209, was commissioned by Henry II, who ordered a stone structure to replace previous rickety wooden bridges. Looking somewhat like the Ponte Vecchio in Florence, there were shops all along London Bridge, on both sides, and in the middle was a chapel dedicated to Thomas à Becket. Ironically, the number of shops and traders meant access was limited, and people complained that it could take an hour to cross the bridge. In 1212, a fire in Southwark spread to the bridge, trapping thousands of people and forcing them to jump into the river. In 1831, John Rennie was commissioned to design a new bridge, constructed in granite. It was the pride of London for many decades – until it was realized that it was sinking. In the 1960s, London Bridge was sold to an American businessman for nearly £2.5 million, and replaced by a concrete-and-steel bridge that opened in 1973.

BRIDGE TRIVIA

- The first suspension bridge across the Thames was built in 1827 at Hammersmith; it was replaced in 1887 by Joseph Bazalgette's suspension bridge.
- Next to Blackfriars Bridge are a group of mysterious red columns: the remains of the London, Chatham & Dover Railway Bridge (1864).
- In the 1880s, Charles Dickens Jr (son of the novelist) published an annual *Dictionary of London*. In 1882, he included this entry: "Alexandra Bridge is a hideous iron structure put together by the L.C.&D. Company to carry their line to Ludgate-hill and the Holborn viaduct. It consists of long lines of gigantic lattice-work girders, inside of which the trains run, and which rest on rows of naked round iron cylinders."
- Visitors to London are often bemused by locals speaking of "The Wobbly Bridge". It's the nickname of Millennium Bridge, a footbridge across the river from near St Paul's Cathedral to Tate Modern and Shakespeare's Globe. The bridge was opened on 10 June 2000 – and closed just three days later. As hundreds of people crowded on, the structure had started to sway. Alarmed, the engineers investigated, raised an extra £5 million and reopened the bridge – minus the wobble – in February 2002.
- In 2014, the new Blackfriars Railway Bridge was unveiled – it was hailed as the largest solar-panel-covered bridge in the world.

Earth has not anything to show more fair:
Dull would he be of soul who could pass by
A sight so touching in its majesty:
This City now doth, like a garment, wear
The beauty of the morning; silent, bare,
Ships, towers, domes, theatres, and temples lie
Open unto the fields, and to the sky;
All bright and glittering in the smokeless air.
Never did sun more beautifully steep
In his first splendour, valley, rock, or hill;
Ne'er saw I, never felt, a calm so deep!
The river glideth at his own sweet will:
Dear God! the very houses seem asleep;
And all that mighty heart is lying still!

William Wordsworth, "Composed upon Westminster Bridge,
September 3, 1802"

FAMOUS LONDON BRIDGES

- Albert Bridge (1873)
- Barnes Bridge (1895)
- Battersea Bridge (1890)
- Blackfriars Railway Bridge (2014)
- Chelsea Bridge (1937)
- Chiswick Bridge (1933)
- Golden Jubilee Bridge (2002)
- Hammersmith Bridge (1887)
- Hungerford Railway Bridge (1864)
- Kew Bridge (1903)
- London Bridge (1932)
- London Bridge (1973)
- Millennium Bridge (2002)
- Putney Bridge (1886)
- Richmond Bridge (1774)
- Southwark Bridge (1921)
- Tower Bridge (1894)
- Twickenham Bridge (1933)

- Vauxhall Bridge (1906)
- Wandsworth Bridge (1940)
- Westminster Bridge (1862)
- Westminster Bridge (1945)

LONDON FACTS

Inside Gray's Antiques Market, near Bond Street, is a small flowing river, alleged to be a part of the lost River Tyburn.

THE DOCKS

By the eighteenth century, the Thames was so busy with shipping traffic that the river could no longer cope. Merchants were livid that river traffic jams meant their ships were stuck for days, unable to unload cargo – and becoming targets for gangs of thieves. As a solution, the West India Docks were built; they opened on 27 August 1802 as the city's first docks built specifically for cargo. There were two dock basins: one for unloading goods from overseas, and the other for loading products to be exported. The West India Docks were soon restricted to handling only goods brought from or heading to the West Indies, and other docks were built, each with its own purpose. The Millwall Docks (1868) were for corn and grain, a trade that had increased following the repeal of the controversial Corn Laws. Other docks were the Victoria Docks (1855) – the first to be linked to railways – and the Royal Albert Dock (1880), for the new breed of iron steam ships. In 1889, the Great Dock Strike saw dockworkers successfully defend their bid for higher wages and better working conditions.

LONDON FACTS

Of the nine warehouses built for the West India Docks, seven were destroyed by bombs in World War II. One of the remaining warehouses is now home to the Museum of London in Docklands.

THE QUEEN'S JUBILEE PAGEANT

In 2012, Queen Elizabeth II's Golden Jubilee was marked with, among other celebrations, a very waterlogged, chilly river pageant. A thousand boats from all over the world joined the Queen's magnificent Elizabethan-style golden barge, *The Spirit of Chartwell*, to process along the Thames, on what happened to be one of the rainiest days of the year. The pageant boats travelled from Hammersmith to Greenwich. Despite the unseasonal weather, over a million people lined the banks of the river to watch.

LONDON FACTS

The Thames takes its name from the Celtic word *tamesas*, which meant "dark".

LONDON'S LOST RIVERS

There are many lost and forgotten waterways in London, mostly now subterranean or dry as their sources have been re-routed. The most famous are:

- Effra
- Fleet
- Tyburn
- Walbrook
- Westbourne

LONDON FACTS

The Westbourne River had to be re-routed around Sloane Square station in a pipe; it runs above a platform.

SPAS OF OLD LONDON

- In the eighteenth century, Acton was a small village outside London but visited regularly for Acton Wells, a popular spa.
- Bayswater was the site of natural springs which provided drinking water for the many working horses that drew carriages on the road between London and Oxford.
- In 1770, a well was discovered in Bermondsey and the area quickly became fashionable as Bermondsey Spa.
- St Bridget's Well was an ancient sacred well, whose name changed over the years to become Bridewell. The name was then used for the palace and prison built on the site – and became known as a generic term for a prison throughout Britain.
- Clerkenwell was the site of a medicinal spring, famous from the twelfth century onwards. The actual well is now beneath an office block on Farringdon Road.
- In the early eighteenth century, Hampstead became famed for the discovery of a well of medicinal waters. A pump room was built and the spa became a popular destination for invalids and tourists.
- Ladywell is named after a scared spring dedicated to the Virgin Mary.
- In the late 1600s, Lambeth became fashionable for Lambeth Wells.
- Muswell Hill is named after a holy well dedicated to the Virgin Mary. It was part of the land given to the nuns of St Mary's priory.
- Spa Fields was once the site of the "London Spaw", initially an ancient spring whose water was considered medically healing, and then of a tavern called the London Spaw, set up in the 1680s to capitalize on the spring. In the eighteenth century it became a fashionable health spa.
- Wells Park in Sydenham was home to an important medicinal spring, discovered in the 1600s.
- Well Walk in Hampstead recalls the fashionable Hampstead Wells spa, first recorded in the late seventeenth century.

TURKISH BATHS

In 1913, the Hotel Russell near Russell Square opened an opulent Turkish-bath spa. There is still a sign set into a nearby pavement, directing would-be customers to the baths that no longer exist (they were demolished in the 1960s). In the 1920s and 1930s, Turkish baths became fashionable all over London. The most famous were Porchester Spa in Bayswater, York Hall in Bethnal Green and Ironmonger Row Baths in Islington.

LIDOS

The first decades of the twentieth century saw a rise in the popularity of outdoor swimming, and lidos were built all over London. There were already several outdoor pools and public baths, including those built at Alexandra Palace in the 1870s. Most lidos became derelict by the 1960s, but some have been rediscovered and reopened, including:

- Brockwell Lido
- Finchley Lido
- London Fields Lido
- Parliament Hill Lido
- Richmond Pools
- The Serpentine Lido
- Tooting Bec Lido

LONDON FACTS

In 1864, the Serpentine Swimming Club was formed and began swimming in the lake in Hyde Park. The Serpentine Lido was opened in 1931, largely thanks to George Lansbury, MP, Commissioner of Works and a social reformer. The lido is open to the public from June to September, but the club's members swim in the lake all year round. They hold events, including the Peter Pan Christmas Day race, which takes place regardless of the water's temperature.

12

LONDON MISCELLANY

THE LONDON AMPHITHEATRE AND FORUM

Beneath the Guildhall in the City of London lie the last remaining stones of a Roman amphitheatre. It was largely destroyed after the Romans left Britain in the fourth century AD, when its stones were used as building materials. The amphitheatre's existence was unknown for almost two millennia before it was discovered in 1988 by a team of archaeologists. For a century, historians and archaeologists had been searching for its site. The Romans also built a forum, in about AD 70, around the same date as the amphitheatre. It lay between present-day Fenchurch, Lombard and Leadenhall streets. There was also a Roman fort close to where the Museum of London stands today.

THE GREAT STINK

In the long, hot summer of 1858, the usual bad smell from the Thames became unbearable. As the heatwave continued, the stench grew so intense that Londoners who could afford to do so left the city, to escape what had become known as the Great Stink.

For centuries the Thames had been used as a rubbish dump and sewer, and as the size and population of the city had grown, the river had become increasingly clogged and revolting. Nearby businesses and public buildings were closed down by the noxious smell. Attempting to ignore the problem, Parliament continued holding sessions, trying to mask the odour from the river outside its windows by ordering servants to hang up sheets soaked in lime chloride, but the Great Stink proved so pervasive that both the House of Commons and House of Lords were closed. In less than a month, MPs agreed to a new system of sewers beneath London – something that sanitary campaigners had been lobbying about for decades.

> *...the state of the Father of English rivers is fast becoming, both in a scientific and social point of view, a matter of national much more than of merely local interest.... The Courts of Law at Westminster are, as the reports inform us, rendered almost intolerable by the stench. The Houses of Parliament can no more be ventilated, for the last chamber from which wholesome air could be poured into them, has itself been seized with the deadly vapour. The steamers on the river are deserted. Watermen are hourly carried to the Hospital.... The whole of the vast body of water rolling upward and downward with every change of tide through the city of London, is not merely charged with putrid animal and vegetable matter, but is actually in a state of putrid fermentation. The stench is, we are told by those who have been near it, fearful ... should this state of things continue a month or two longer, something like a pestilence may be expected to break out in the Metropolis.*

> **Leeds Mercury, 1 July 1858**

LONDON FACTS

London was the first city in Roman Britain to mint coins. A London mint was founded in AD 288 – so that the Roman troops could be paid.

QUEEN VICTORIA'S FUNERAL

It was in no sense a sad occasion – it was far too solemn to be melancholy. Hours before the pageant passed its route was packed and lined with the greatest multitude that any living person has seen in London. From on all sides people poured towards the scene of the procession; the sound of wheels was silent and the streets resounded only with the tramping of feet. At points such as the railway stations and Buckingham Palace the crowd seemed to expand into seas of living faces. In the time of waiting the people talked quietly and cheerfully among themselves, interested in the forming up of the troops, and ready to be amused in a quiet way by the little incidents that enliven such intervals. There was no false restraint, no attempt to beat up artificial emotion. It was a silent crowd; indeed its supreme characteristics were its blackness and silence. People were silent because they wished to be silent, because the magnetism of the hour was upon them, and its solemnity. Shutting one's eyes, it was the seashore that seemed to sound – not the busy city with its clamorous voices and roarings.

Over London there hung the light mist of our winter mornings, and the sun shone like a dim, far-off lighthouse, with its intervals of eclipse. When the dead Queen's body was borne past, the silence simply deepened – that was all.

Manchester Guardian, 4 February 1901

JEREMY BENTHAM'S AUTO ICON

In 1832, the philosopher and social reformer Jeremy Bentham died. In his will, he requested that he should be turned into an "auto icon", meaning that his body should be preserved and presented as a sculpture. Today he still sits on a chair in University College London's South Cloisters. He is dressed in his own clothes and the body is his – but the embalmers were unable preserve the head, so the auto icon has a wax copy instead.

An excerpt from Bentham's will:

My body I give to my dear friend Doctor Southwood Smith.... The skeleton he will cause to be put together in such a manner as that the whole figure may be seated in a chair usually occupied by me when living, in the attitude in which I am sitting when engaged in thought in the course of time employed in writing. I direct that the body thus prepared shall be transferred to my executor. He will cause the skeleton to be clad in one of the suits of black occasionally worn by me.

THE HORSE HOSPITAL

In the final years of the eighteenth century, architect James Burton built a mews – a place where working animals (such as carriage horses or hunting birds) were kept. It became a horse hospital, a vital service in a city where so many businesses relied on horsepower. Today, the architecture remains true to the design of the equine hospital, but houses arts spaces and The Contemporary Wardrobe Collection, an eclectic selection of fashion dating from 1947 onwards, which is hired by film, TV and fashion companies.

THE WHITECHAPEL BELL FOUNDRY

This foundry in east London is the oldest manufacturing business in Britain, active continually since 1570. One of its most famous products is Big Ben, for the Palace of Westminster, cast in 1858. This remains the largest bell that the foundry has ever produced, weighing 13.5 tons. It also made the Liberty Bell (1752) now in Philadelphia, USA, a set of 12 bells for Toronto Cathedral in Canada, and the very first set of handbells to be sent to America. The current building dates from 1670. The foundry has an exhibition space, which serves as a little museum, and offers guided tours.

ZEPPELIN AHOY!

The first attack on London in World War I was from a German zeppelin, on the night of 31 May to 1 June 1915. The first place hit was a residential street in Stoke Newington, then the bomber moved on to attack Shoreditch, Stepney and Leytonstone. Seven people died and dozens were injured.

LONDON FACTS

On the eve of World War II, the average life expectancy of a Londoner was 62 years. In 2015, the average life expectancy of a Londoner was 82 years.

SMOG

From the early years of the Industrial Revolution in the eighteenth century, through to the mid-1900s, London was notorious for its thick blanket of smog which often hung over the city even on the hottest and sunniest of days. Particularly thick, dangerous smog was reported in 1813, 1873, 1880, 1882, 1891, 1892 and 1948. The deadliest smog of the twentieth century, on 5–9 December 1952, killed thousands of people and brought public transport to a standstill. Media reports claimed that cattle in Smithfield market suffocated. This final fatal smog led directly to the Clean Air Acts of 1956 and 1968, which changed the type of fuel allowed to be burnt in various parts of the country where smog had been a problem. Central London became part of the "smokeless zone", where only authorized fuel types that don't produce much smoke can be burnt – so burning wood was banned. This is why so many London homes have bricked-up fireplaces.

The sky is cloudy, yellowed by the smoke.
For view there are the houses opposite
Cutting the sky with one long line of wall
Like solid fog: far as the eye can stretch
Monotony of surface & of form
Without a break to hang a guess upon.
No bird can make a shadow as it flies,
For all is shadow, as in ways o'erhung
By thickest canvass, where the golden rays
Are clothed in hemp. No figure lingering
Pauses to feed the hunger of the eye
Or rest a little on the lap of life.
All hurry on & look upon the ground,
Or glance unmarking at the passers by.
The wheels are hurrying too, cabs, carriages
All closed, in multiplied identity.
The world seems one huge prison-house & court
Where men are punished at the slightest cost,
With lowest rate of colour, warmth & joy.

George Eliot, "In a London Drawing Room"

LONDON'S FIRST ESCALATOR

In 1898, a new form of technology reached Britain from America. The first moving staircase or "escalator" in London was installed in Harrods department store. On 16 November 1898 the *Morning Post* recorded the occasion in its Notices: "Opening of the New Patent 'Moving Staircase' at Harrod's, 87 to 105, Brompton-road, at one o'clock". Harrods staff were detailed to stand at the top of the escalator and hand out tots of brandy to nervous customers. Within a year, the sensation had become a tourist destination. On 19 December 1899, the *Pall Mall Gazette* wrote:

> *It is small wonder that the children are revelling just not in the joys of the Christmas Bazaar at Harrod's Stores, in Brompton-road, and begging to be taken there again and again, if only for the sake of making that thrilling ascent on the wonderful moving staircase, a joy which never seems to pall on the juvenile visitors, and in which the "grown-ups" also appear to take a keen delight.*

THE WHALE IN THE THAMES

On the early morning of 20 January 2006, a lone northern bottlenose whale was spotted swimming in the River Thames. Members of the British Divers Marine Life Rescue group made attempts to save her, but she was obviously distressed and disoriented, and died from convulsions on the evening of 21 January. While she was in the Thames, thousands of Londoners lined the Embankment and other riverside streets, standing in silence so as not to scare the whale. This was the first time a whale had been recorded in the Thames, but dolphins and porpoises have been sighted occasionally. In 2013, a school of harbour porpoises swam through central London. The Marine Policing Unit tweeted a picture and the comment, "The porpoises seem happy enough. They are surfacing regularly and are staying in the Westminster area."

LONDON'S WHALING HISTORY

- London was once embroiled in the whaling industry. In 1608, a 60-tonne whaling ship was sent to Spitzbergen to hunt for right whales. Soon there was a fleet of 12 whalers owned by London whaling companies.
- These whaling ships left from Howland Dock, soon known as the Greenland Dock.
- The last whaler ship sent from London was the *Margaret*, which was lost in severe weather and ice in 1836.
- Whaling could be a lucrative business because of the voracious desire by Europeans for whale oil – used to lubricate machinery, as lamp oil and to make soap, candles and other domestic items.
- "Whalebone" was also highly prized, as it was used for women's corsets. It is not actually bone but baleen, the sieve-like feeding plates in the mouths of baleen whales, which is made of keratin.
- It is likely that the mythical unicorn was inspired by whalers bringing back the tusks of narwhals.
- In 1658 a right whale was spotted swimming near Deptford – and harpooned. Its death was seen as evocative of the death of Oliver Cromwell. Whalebone Lane in E15 is named after it.

13

LONDON TRADITIONS

FROST FAIRS

Before the Thames had so many bridges and when the river was much wider, it did not flow as fast as it does today and would occasionally freeze over completely. London was much colder before the population grew so big, before houses with fireplaces were prevalent. Between 1607 and 1814 there were seven recorded large frost fairs on the Thames; there was also ice-skating and other sports on the frozen river.

MAYPOLES

London was once home to several maypoles (traditionally erected in May), including one on The Strand (at the site of St Mary le Strand) said to be 9 m (30 ft) tall. When the Puritans came to power, maypoles were banned as a symbol of Pagan times when Britons worshiped trees. Following the Restoration of the monarchy, a 12-m (40-ft) maypole was re-erected on The Strand. It was later moved to near Somerset House.

LONDON FACTS

The first mention of a Punch and Judy show is in the diary of Samuel Pepys, on 9 May 1662. He saw it at Covent Garden.

COCKNEYS

Cockney rhyming slang was born in the East End of London. It constantly evolved with political and social change, and sometimes varied from street to street and family to family.

- apples and pears = stairs
- Mother Hubbard = cupboard
- bacon and eggs = legs
- loaf of bread = head
- donkeys' ears = years
- rabbit and pork = talk
- tea leaf = thief
- porky pie = lie
- Harry Lime = time
- Auntie Nelly/Derby Kelly/New Delhi = belly

Pearly Kings and Queens date back to the nineteenth century from costermongers' fairs where a "Coster King and Queen" would be chosen. The first full pearly costume was worn in the 1880s by Harry Croft.

LONDON FACTS

A true Cockney must be born within the sound of Bow Bells (the bells of St-Mary-le-Bow Church).

OTHER NOTABLE TRADITIONS

- The Grimaldi Service is held every year on the first Sunday in February at a church in east London. Scores of clowns gather together to remember the pioneer of clowning Joseph Grimaldi (1778–1837).
- Every December since 1947, the people of Norway have sent a gigantic Christmas tree to the people of London, to be displayed in Trafalgar Square. It is in thanks for the help given to Norway during World War II, including allowing the country's freedom fighters to base themselves in London.

14

TRANSPORT

London increases every day ... I believe you will think the town cannot hold all its inhabitants, so prodigiously the population is augmented. I have twice been going to stop my coach in Piccadilly (and the same has happened to Lady Ailesbury), thinking there was a mob, and it was only nymphs and swains sauntering or trudging. T'other morning, i.e., at two o'clock, I went to see Mrs. Garrick and Miss Hannah More at the Adelphi, and was stopped five times before I reached Northumberland House; for the tides of coaches, chariots, curricles, phaetons, &c., are endless. Indeed, the town is so extended, that the breed of chairs is almost lost; for Hercules and Atlas could not carry anybody from one end of the enormous capital to the other. How magnified would be the error of the young woman at St. Helena, who some years ago said to the captain of an Indiaman, "I suppose London is very empty when the India ships come out".

Horace Walpole, letter to Miss Berry, 18 April 1791

RIVER TRANSPORT

For centuries, London was one of the most important ports in the world; by the end of the 1700s, it was also the busiest. From the beginning, invaders – including Romans and Vikings – arrived by sea and sailed up the Thames; immigrants also arrived from all over the globe. Until the mid-twentieth century, the Thames was a heavily polluted working river, the most important transport link in London, with merchant ships constantly setting sail to export and import goods worldwide.

For centuries, watermen ran small wooden boats known as "wherries", which were London's earliest version of a taxi, similar to gondolas in Venice, taking passengers up and down the river and, as London had very few bridges until the nineteenth century, across it. Wherries were painted in bright colours and patterns, to distinguish one family business from another. Thames watermen could become famous through the races they ran regularly on the river to prove their superiority over rival operators.

> *Ocean craft run here in great numbers, as it is a safe harbour. I myself saw one large ship after another over the whole city's length, from St Catherine's suburb to the Bridge, some hundred vessels in all.*
>
> **From the letters of Swiss traveller Thomas Platter, who visited London in 1599**

THE THAMES TUNNEL

Although Isambard Kingdom Brunel remains famous today, few people have heard of his father, Marc Brunel. He was a French emigré and brilliant inventor, who worked with his son on a number of important projects, most famously the Thames Tunnel. What the Brunels had wanted to build was a Channel Tunnel, linking Britain and France, but Queen Victoria's government was reluctant to give the go-ahead, for fear that a tunnel beneath the English Channel would enable the French to invade. Construction of the Thames Tunnel was difficult and dangerous: several workers died and Isambard almost drowned. It took to decades to build, but the Thames Tunnel opened in 1843. Although intended for horse-drawn carriages, it was only used by pedestrians until trains began to use it in 1869. It remains part of the London Transport system today.

> *The Thames Tunnel is now open for the transit of passengers. Another wonder has been added to the many of which London can boast; another triumph been achieved by British enterprize [sic], genius, and perseverance.*
>
> **"Opening the Thames Tunnel", *Morning Chronicle*, 27 March 1843**

RAILWAYS

- In 1808, there was a demonstration of steam locomotion in Euston.
- In 1833, Parliament authorized London's first railway line, from London Bridge to Greenwich. The first section began service in 1836 – before either station was completed.
- Londoners were rapidly persuaded to try the new trains as they were faster than taxi carriages, wherries and steamboats.
- The London to Croydon Railway opened in 1839 and the London to Brighton Railway in 1841; soon there were railway lines running from London all over the country.
- Many of today's trains still run on the original routes.

> *The first shock of a great earthquake had, just at that period, rent the whole neighbourhood to its centre. Traces of its course were visible on every side. Houses were knocked down; streets broken through and stopped; deep pits and trenches dug in the ground; enormous heaps of earth and clay thrown up; buildings that were undermined and shaking, propped by great beams of wood. Here, a chaos of carts, overthrown and jumbled together, lay topsy-turvy at the bottom of a steep unnatural hill; there, confused treasures of iron soaked and rusted in something that had accidentally become a pond. Everywhere were bridges that led nowhere; throughfares that were wholly impassable; Babel towers of chimneys, wanting half their height; temporary wooden houses and enclosures, in the most unlikely situations; carcases of ragged tenements, and fragments of unfinished walls and arches, and piles of scaffolding, and wildernesses of bricks, and giant forms of cranes, and tripods straddling above nothing.... In short, the yet unfinished and unopened Railroad was in progress.*
>
> **Charles Dickens, *Dombey and Son*, 1848**

RAILWAY STATIONS

In the nineteenth century, the arrival of the railways changed London's landscape forever. Just as the Crossrail project started to rip up the heart of many historic London properties in the 2000s, in the mid-1800s the building of railways and their stations changed the city entirely. Among the most celebrated early stations are:

- London Bridge (1836)
- Euston (1837)
- Fenchurch Street (1841)
- Waterloo (1848)
- King's Cross (1852)
- Paddington (1854)
- Victoria (1860)

- Charing Cross (1864)
- Cannon Street (1866)
- St Pancras (1868)
- Liverpool Street (1871)
- Blackfriars (1886)
- Marylebone (1889)

RAILWAY STATION FACTS

- The first of London's railway stations was London Bridge.
- The last of the major stations to be built was Marylebone.
- In its first year, London Bridge station was visited by around half a million travellers. By the 1840s, over two million passengers a year were using it.
- Around 3,000 people were evicted from their homes so that Fenchurch Street station could be built.
- Many of the stations have been rebuilt since their Victorian incarnations. Notoriously, Euston's regal nineteenth-century station was knocked down in the 1960s and replaced by an unpopular new building.
- Victoria station was named after Queen Victoria. Before the introduction of air travel and Eurostar, the "boat train" from Victoria was the fashionable (and expensive) method of travelling between London and Paris.
- Marylebone station is one of the most filmed locations in London and has appeared in adverts, films and TV productions including *Agatha Christie's Marple*, *Gavin & Stacey*, *Spooks*, *A Hard Day's Night* and *The Ipcress File*.
- By 1900, London had more railway termini than any other city in the world.
- King's Cross takes its name from a monument to King George IV, which once stood near the site. The station's fictional "Platform 9$^3/_4$" from the Harry Potter novels, is now commemorated on the concourse.
- Paddington station was built specifically for Isambard Kingdom Brunel's new train service, the Great Western Railway. The timetable brought about a change in British life: the regulation of all clocks and timing around the country. When the railway first opened, there was around

30 minutes' difference between the time in London and that in Bristol. Paddington station today has statues of both Brunel and children's-fiction favourite Paddington Bear, named after the station.

LONDON FACTS

In 1862, the artist William Powell Frith painted *The Railway Station*, based largely on photographs of Paddington station, designed by Brunel. Among the throng of figures in the station, Frith and his family are recognizable.

EUROSTAR

On 6 May 1994, Queen Elizabeth II declared Waterloo International station open, then boarded the first Eurostar train to France, where she met President Mitterrand. The Channel Tunnel was officially open – 151 years after the Brunels had opened the Thames Tunnel. In November 2007, the Eurostar terminal moved to St Pancras.

LONDON OVERGROUND

In 2007, a new rail network was opened in London, the Overground, connecting previously distant boroughs and eliminating the need for multiple changes. The Watford Junction to Euston branch of the Overground runs along the route of one of the oldest railway lines in Britain, the London and Birmingham Line, which opened in 1838.

BUSES

Until the 1820s, the only public transport options were expensive and unreliable: stage coaches and hackney carriages, as well as sedan chairs for hire by the wealthy on short journeys. A proper public transport system was much needed. Shillibeer's Omnibus began a service between Paddington and Bank, on 4 July 1829, for a shilling. It was an immediate success, permitting far more people to afford transport across the city. An early poster advertising the omnibus described it as "a new carriage on the Parisian mode, for the conveyance of inside passengers". Shillibeer found himself in fierce competition with a huge number of new omnibus operators, all wanting to cash in on his success. Soon there were omnibus routes offered all over London.

Until 1832, it was forbidden for omnibuses to work in the City, as hackney carriages still had a monopoly. After the law was changed, a new age of the horse-drawn omnibus began. An important pioneer was Thomas Tilling, who is credited with setting up London's oldest bus service, in 1846. (The company continued, run by the Tilling family, until 1948.) Ten years later, in 1856, the London General Omnibus Company was set up, taking over several independent operators. Within a year it owned even more operators and 600 vehicles. Passengers now had several options and ticket-buying power, making competition fierce. Buses began to be regulated and timetables appeared.

BUS FACTS

- Almost from the start, omnibuses were considered ideal for advertisements, and placards appeared on every bit of available space.
- In 1891, the motor bus appeared in London. The first route was between Victoria and Charing Cross, on which the buses travelled at a speed of 13 km/h (8 mph).
- Night buses were introduced in 1909.
- In 1920 the K-type motor bus appeared.
- The first covered double-decker bus dates from the 1920s.
- During the General Strike of 1926, entrepreneurs began running independent buses on routes where affected buses should have been.
- The first Routemaster bus was seen on the streets of London in 1956.
- Early Routemaster buses were green – not the now-iconic red.
- For the Queen's Silver Jubilee in 1977, 25 London buses were painted silver.

WOMEN AND BUSES

In 1846, a female entrepreneur made her mark on the London bus scene. Her name was Elizabeth Birch, better known as "the widow Birch", and she set up the Westminster Omnibus association, turning what had been her husband's small business into a family empire. Despite this early female pioneer, other women were discriminated against throughout the bus service until well into the late twentieth century. Although women took over most London transport jobs during World War II, once the war was over they were still banned from applying to be drivers, having to content themselves with working as conductors or "clippies". In 1974, the law changed, permitting women to apply for any job. In the same year, the first female bus driver was seen on the streets of London; her name was Jill Viner.

LONDON FACTS

A new bus appeared in the 1860s, known as a Knifeboard omnibus. The "knifeboard" was a type of bench placed on top of the omnibus, to permit seating on the roof: an open-topped double-decker. This was a solution to overcrowding, popular on sunny days but not in wind and rain.

TRAMS

In 1861, an American businessman with the appropriate name of George Train brought the first trams to London. He ran three experimental lines (in Victoria, Bayswater and from Westminster Bridge to Kennington). These horse-drawn trams were greatly disliked, and the tram lines, so irritating to pedestrians and other road users, were dismantled within a few months. Yet just nine years later, a horse-drawn tram service began between Kennington and Brixton. The technology of tram lines had been greatly improved, making them much more discreet and less of a hazard for people and horses. Tickets cost a penny per mile and the trams travelled at up to 10 km/h (6 mph). The rails meant that horses pulling trams could move faster than those pulling omnibuses.

LONDON FACTS

By the end of the nineteenth century, London's public transport system used around 50,000 horses. They were housed at Mare St stables in Hackney.

TAXIS

The first hackney carriages for hire were seen in London during the reign of Elizabeth I – carriages were expensive to run, so wealthy owners spread the costs by hiring them out to people who couldn't afford to own one. The first traceable cab rank in London was set up in 1634, by a soldier and explorer named Captain John Baily. He had a fleet of four coaches for hire, which waited for customers beside the maypole on The Strand. By the mid-eighteenth century, carriages for hire could be seen all over London, and by the early nineteenth, customers could choose between nifty two-wheeled carriages and larger, more spacious cabs for a big group of passengers. At the end of the Victorian age, electric motor cabs had been trialled and failed; within a few years, petrol cabs started appearing. The taxi trade suffered huge losses during both world wars, and it was recognized that something needed to be done, not least because most London cabs were, by this date, old and unreliable models of car. In 1948, the Austin FX3 was introduced, and from then onwards the London taxi began to thrive.

HACKNEY CARRIAGES

Up to the eighteenth century, the most common method of road transportation was a horse-drawn, four-wheeled vehicle called a hackney carriage. The word comes not from the London borough of Hackney but from the French name for a type of horse, *hacquenée*.

TAXI TRIVIA

- The word "cab" comes from the French word *cabriolet*, a popular two-wheeled carriage that came to London in the late Georgian era.
- The word "taxi" comes from the "taximeter" – in 1907 it became compulsory for all cabs to have meters fitted, to stop customers being overcharged.
- In 1907, a navigation test for London cabbies was introduced. Known today as "The Knowledge", it can take three to four years to learn.
- In 1958, the now-iconic Austin FX4 taxi was seen for the first time.
- The first minicabs appeared in London in 1961 – cab wars ensued on the streets, with minicabs touting for black cabs' customers and black cabs deliberately blocking minicabs so they couldn't move.

THE TUBE

The Tube is the world's oldest underground railway. The first line was opened on 10 January 1863; it was the Metropolitan Line, between present-day Paddington and Farringdon stations. An estimated 30,000 passengers used the line on that first day. In 1863, Paddington was known as Bishop's Road station. Today there are 270 Tube stations. There are also a large number of "ghost" Tube stations, formerly operational but now closed down. Several have been used as locations in films and TV programmes, most famously in James Bond films.

TUBE BABIES

In 1924, the first baby was born on the Tube, at Elephant and Castle. She was named Marie Cordery – although several newspapers ran erroneous stories crediting her with names that began with the initials T.U.B.E. A second baby girl was born on the Tube in December 2008, at Kingsbury station. Just a few months later, in May 2009, the first baby boy was born on the Tube, in the staff room at London Bridge.

TUBE FACTS

- The first Tube trains ran on steam.
- In 1890, the world's first deep-level electric railway was opened, connecting the suburb of Stockwell with the City of London. It was known as The City and South London Railway.
- In 1902, an American financier, Charles Tyson Yerkes, helped save the Tube system from bankruptcy.
- Until 1933, the Tube was run by several independent operators. The creation of London Transport brought all the lines together, managed by one organization.
- During World War II, the depth of underground Tube stations made them ideal for use as air-raid shelters.
- Treasures from the nearby British Museum were stored inside Holborn station during World War II.
- Hampstead station has the most steps: 320.

- The Docklands Light Railway was opened in 1987.
- In 2003 a new form of Tube ticket was issued: the Oyster card.
- Since 2009 the Circle Line has no longer been circular: the line was extended along the route of the Hammersmith & City Line to Hammersmith, meaning it is no longer possible to ride around the Circle Line without changing trains.
- Kings Cross St Pancras station connects more Underground lines than any other station.
- The famous Tube logo – now copied all over the world – was first seen in 1908. The orange Overground sign is based on it.

LONDON FACTS

When children's charity founder Dr Thomas Barnardo died on 19 September 1905, aged 60, he was given a public funeral. Thousands of people, including hundreds of the children his charity had helped, thronged the streets. His coffin was transported by Tube – the only other person afforded this honour was former Prime Minister William Ewart Gladstone in 1898.

HARRY BECK'S ICONIC MAP

The London Tube map is famous worldwide: it has become a design icon, widely copied. Before the 1930s, London's Tube map was a higgledy-piggledy mess, with most maps showing only a few lines and little understanding of how they connected. That changed in 1931, when engineering draftsman Harry Beck began developing a new design, following several years working for the London Underground Signals Office. Initially, the official response to Beck's map was less than laudatory, as the publicity department for London Underground thought its design much too "radical". Eventually they published a small number of the maps in 1933 to gauge public reaction. It was an immediate success. Beck was paid just eight guineas for his work.

TUBE DISASTERS

- In March 1943, a burst of enemy rockets fired on the East End of London caused tragedy at Bethnal Green Tube station. As people left their homes to shelter inside the station, a crowd massed at the top of the stairs and people were pushed and crushed. So many people fell down the stairs that 173 died.

- On 28 February 1975, an accident on the Northern Line at Moorgate killed 43 people when a train failed to stop and crashed into a wall at the end of the tunnel.

- In 1987, 31 people were killed and many more injured in a fire at King's Cross Tube station. More than 150 firefighters fought the blaze, one of whom lost his life in the fire. The conflagration was believed to have been started by a discarded match. A number of safety measures were instituted after the fire, including a smoking ban on Tube stations (smoking had been banned on trains in 1984) and the removal of wooden escalators.

- On 7 July 2005, terrorists targeted London's public transport system. Three simultaneous bombs were detonated on Tube trains near Liverpool Street, Edgware Road and King's Cross/Russell Square stations. A fourth bomb exploded on a bus in Tavistock Square, Bloomsbury. In addition to the suicide bombers themselves, 52 people were killed and more than 700 injured by the explosions.

LONDON FACTS

In 1911, the first Tube station escalator was installed. It was at Earls Court and caused great excitement – and fear. To overcome public qualms over the new technology, a one-legged man was hired to ride on the escalator all day, to prove how safe and easy it was. William "Bumper" Harris was an engineer who had lost his leg in an accident. The London Transport Museum owns in its collection a silver pocket watch given to Harris by his wife as a wedding present; he was wearing it on the day he spent hours on the Earls Court escalator. The museum also owns a walking stick used by Harris, who – as an engineer – was Clerk of Works for the installation of the escalators at Charing Cross in 1913. It was made from the wood of an ancient oak tree discovered more than 15 m (50 ft) below the city during the excavation of the station, a depth that is testimony to how much the streets of London had been built up since the city's earliest settlement.

15

MARKETS

POPULAR LONDON MARKETS

Alfie's
Bayswater Road
Bermondsey
Billingsgate
Borough Market
Brick Lane
Brixton
Camden
Chapel Market
Columbia Road
Covent Garden
Gray's Antique Market
Greenwich
Leadenhall Market
Leather Lane
Petticoat Lane
Piccadilly (at St James's Church)
Portobello
Shepherd's Bush
Smithfield
Spitalfields

Columbia Road's original market was established by Angela Burdett-Coutts in a philanthropic attempt to persuade market traders off the streets and into a proper market. It was shortlived, but the flower market remains in its place.

FAMOUS LONDONERS

Angela Burdett-Coutts (1814–1906) was the unexpected heiress of the fortune of her grandfather, Thomas Coutts, founder of Coutts bank. She was one of the wealthiest women in the world – and a philanthropist, establishing housing projects, giving money to widows, funding hospitals, paying pensions to disabled soldiers and providing clean drinking water for poor people in London. In 1851, she gave an interest-free loan to the founder of the Royal Marsden Hospital as she was a fervent supporter of his cancer research work. She also provided the RNLI with lifeboats, funded the RSPCA and NSPCC, gave money to help Charles Babbage in his computer work and founded a house with Charles Dickens to rehabilitate "fallen women". In the East End she became known as "the queen of the poor".

The name Aldwych derives from the main market of Lundenwic, which became known as *ealdwic*, meaning "old settlement". At that date, the area now known as Aldwych was on the banks of the river and the many of the market traders sold their goods from boats.

LONDON FACTS

Millbank Penitentiary was built to replace the prison ships, or "hulks", and designed on principles espoused by the philospher Jeremy Bentham. The prisoners at Millbank had been sentenced to Transportation, and were awaiting the prison ships bound for Australia. Millbank Penitentiary was opened in 1816 to a radical new design known as a Panopticon, with the prisoners' cells spanning out from a central building that housed the governors and guards, allowing the guards to keep an eye on the prisoners at all times, and giving the prisoners the impression that they were being watched. The prison closed in 1890. The Tate Britain now stands on part of the land that housed the prison.

16

LONDON'S LOST COFFEE AND CHOCOLATE HOUSES

COFFEE HOUSES

In the seventeenth and eighteenth centuries, London was renowned for its coffee houses. After the first coffee house in Britain opened in Oxford, the fashion quickly spread to London. Soon coffee houses became recognized as places where businessmen met: no women were allowed and, usually, no alcohol was served. Coffee had begun to be marketed as a brain food, recognized as a stimulant. Coffee houses were much more appropriate meeting places than the traditional taverns, where business meetings often descended into drunken arguments. Today, nothing remains of the old London coffee houses, except for the few surviving clubs that grew out of them – and the many businesses that evolved, the most famous of which is Lloyd's of London. Coffee houses were not only places of business, however, and soon developed a reputation for hard gambling. In 1724, the Scottish traveller (and spy) John Macky wrote:

> *I am lodged in the street Pall-Mall, the ordinary residence of all strangers, because of its vicinity to the King's Palace, the Park, the Parliament House, the theatres, and the chocolate and coffee-houses, where the best company frequent. If you would know our manner or living, it is thus:– we rise by*

nine ... about twelve, the beau-monde assembles in several chocolate and coffee-houses, the best of which are the Cocoa Tree and White's chocolate-houses, St James's, the Smyrna and the British Coffee-houses; and all these are so near one another, that in less than an hour you see the company of them all. We are carried to these places in chairs, which are here very cheap, a guinea a-week or a shilling an hour; and your chairmen serve you as porters to run on errands, as your gondoliers do at Venice.

THE GREAT COFFEE PROBLEM

The manager of one of London's biggest hotels was discussing the great coffee problem with me yesterday. "You cannot get perfect coffee in London, even here," he said. It was a terrible admission from a manager in his own hotel, and I enquired further. "When this hotel first opened," he explained, "we secured from Vienna probably the finest coffee maker in the world. After a few weeks he resigned, heartbroken, and returned to Austria. He gave as his reason that with London water it was utterly impossible to make coffee worthy of his reputation."

Daily Mirror, 25 February 1914

COFFEE-HOUSE FACTS

- The first documented coffee house in London was opened in 1652 by Pasqua Rosee, a Greek-Sicilian immigrant who had been working as a domestic servant. It was in St Michael's Alley, Cornhill. Today, the site of London's first coffee house is occupied by the Jamaica Wine House.
- Each coffee house became known for its political affiliations, or for attracting people of a certain industry or occupation. Clients were usually fiercely loyal to their own specific coffee house.
- In the 1680s, the coffee house opened by Edward Lloyd began to be recognized as the main meeting place for those involved in the marine industry business.
- The London Stock Exchange had its origins in Jonathan's Coffee House in Exchange Alley.

- Coffee houses also served "gentlemen of leisure": those rich enough not to need an occupation.
- One coffee house which seldom makes it into the history books was that founded by Richard Hogarth (father of the artist William Hogarth). He sank all his savings into a Latin-only-speaking coffee house; he had very few customers.
- Unlike most seventeenth-century institutions, coffee houses were open to men of all social classes.
- In 1675, Charles II made an attempt to ban coffee houses, for fear of subversive societies being set up due to the mixing of the social classes. His proposal caused such an outcry that he was forced to scrap it.
- The once-famous London coffee houses became less lucrative by the end of the eighteenth century, and by the nineteenth century almost none survived. They had been scuppered by the arrival of tea, which had overtaken coffee as a fashionable drink.
- In the mid-nineteenth century, leaders of the Temperance Movement attempted to revive the coffee- and chocolate-house culture, as an attempt to lure men away from pubs. It was not particularly successful.
- In the late twentieth century, café culture reappeared in London – but this time via large groups of imported café chains.
- It took a while for independent London coffee houses to re-emerge but by the start of the twenty-first century they were increasing in popularity.

> *Before 1715, the number of coffee-houses in London was reckoned at two thousand. Every profession, trade, class, party, had its favourite coffee-house. The lawyers discussed law or literature, criticized the last new play or literary work at the coffee-house. Here the young bloods of the Inns of Court paraded their Indian gowns and laced caps of a morning, and swaggered in their laced coats and Mechlin ruffles at night after the Theatre. The cits [sic] met to discuss the rise and fall of stocks, and to settle the rate of insurances …; the parsons exchanged University gossip or commented on Dr. Sacheverell's last sermon.*
>
> *The Era,* 24 October 1880

CHOCOLATE HOUSES

Cocoa beans were first brought to Europe from the Americas during the sixteenth century, and by the seventeenth century the fashion for drinking chocolate was sweeping London – techniques for making it into a solid food had not yet arrived. Drinking chocolate was usually flavoured with exotic spices from all over the world, including cinnamon, vanilla, ambergris, jasmine and musk. It was credited with remarkable powers: as an aphrodisiac (for both men and women), a hangover cure and a cure for dyspeptic stomachs. It was produced almost entirely by slave labour.

Ozinda's chocolate house opened in St James's in 1614 and thrived for over a century. By the mid-eighteenth century it had fallen out of fashion and the building was demolished in 1748. Ozinda's was a Tory meeting place and a popular gambling house. The author Jonathan Swift was a regular visitor, recording in his journal of 1712 a "mighty fine" dinner: "We eat it at Ozinda's Chocolate-house, just by St. James's. We were never merrier, nor better company, and did not part till after eleven." In 1715, however, Ozinda's was raided by the King's soldiers, convinced that Jacobite rebels were plotting there, and several customers were carried off to Newgate Prison.

> *Mr. Ozinda, keeping the Chocolate-house joining to St. James's Gate, being dispos'd to return to France, intends by Auction to sell all his Household Goods and Pictures ... and likewise his Shop Goods, consisting of several Sorts of Snuffs, as old Havana and Seville, etc. with Several Sorts of superfine Liquors of his own making, as Egro de Cedro, Cinamon Water, Piercico, etc. with a Quantity of Hermitage Wine...*
> **The Daily Post, 28 March 1724**

White's chocolate house was also in St James's, founded in 1693; by *c.*1698 it had become so popular that it moved into bigger premises across the road. Some years later it became the notorious White's Club (the oldest gentleman's club in London). William Hogarth was alleged to have used one of the rooms at White's in his famous series paintings *The Rake's Progress* (1733), a morality tale about a man who inherits a fortune but loses it all and ends up a pauper-lunatic in Bedlam. White's remained open to the public for over four decades, before becoming a private members-only club in 1736.

> *All accounts of gallantry, pleasure and entertainment shall*
> *be under the article of White's Chocolate House.*
>> ***Tatler*, 12 April 1709**

The Cocoa Tree chocolate house opened on Pall Mall in the 1690s; its first mention dates from 1698. It was a popular meeting place for Tories, and for some time was considered the Tory Party's headquarters; it was also a notorious gambling den. Its political rival was the St James Coffee House, nearby, which was a Whig meeting place. In later years it was discovered to have housed a secret underground passageway, as it – not Ozinda's – was the main meeting point for Jacobite rebels. It was rumoured to have been visited by Bonnie Prince Charlie (the "Young Pretender") for a meeting with supporters in 1750. In July 1723, the Cocoa Tree was inconvenienced by the collapse of sewers north of Pall Mall, into which half the road fell. The RAC Club now occupies the site of the old Cocoa Tree.

> *My face is very well known at the Grecian, the Cocoa*
> *Tree, and in the theatres.*
>> **Charles Brockden Brown, *The Spectator*, 1 March 1711**

LONDON FACTS

Hampton Court Palace had its own royal chocolate kitchen, deliberately positioned away from the areas where meats and other strong-smelling foods were produced.

17

SPORT

THE OLYMPIC GAMES

London has hosted the Olympic Games three times. The **1908 Olympics** were originally intended to be held in Rome, but after Mount Vesuvius erupted on 7 April 1906 it became apparent that Italy could not afford to pay for both the Olympics and the rebuilding of Naples and its environs. London was asked to take Rome's place, and it was decided to hold the Olympics at the White City exhibition centre, which was being built for the Franco-British Exhibition of 1908.

- The Games were organized by Lord Desborough, who was a climber, rower and swimmer. They were officially opened by King Edward VII.
- The White City was built by George Wimpey in west London. Several years after the Olympics, part of the White City centre was demolished to make way for new BBC buildings.
- The games were the longest in Olympic history, beginning on 27 April and ending on 31 October.
- American flag bearer Ralph Rose caused controversy because he refused to lower his flag in front of the Royal Box.
- Finnish athletes refused to march with a flag after being told that they were expected to march under the flag of occupying Russia.
- Some Swedish athletes declined to take part when it was discovered that the Olympic organizers had forgotten to fly the Swedish flag with all the others.
- 37 women made history by competing in the games.
- 2,000 athletes from 22 countries took part in the 1908 Olympics.

THE 1908 OLYMPIC MARATHON

The length of the marathon had previously been 26 miles (42 km), but at the 1908 Olympics an extra 385 yds (352 m) was added, so that runners – who began at Windsor Castle and finished at White City – could finish in front of the Royal Box. The marathon should have been won by an Italian, Dorando Pietri, as he beat the other runners to the 26-mile (42-km) mark, but he arrived inside the stadium and ran in the wrong direction, then ran in the right direction before collapsing; he got up but collapsed again. A couple of officials ran forward and helped him up and across the finishing line. After complaints from other athletes, he was disqualified because he had received assistance. Queen Alexandra, who had insisted on the extra 385 yds (352 m), felt so guilty that she championed Pietri, personally presenting him with a gold cup and making him a post-Olympic celebrity. Sir Arthur Conan Doyle was at the finishing line, and wrote about it in the *Daily Mail*:

But how different from the exultant victor whom we expected! Out of the dark archway there staggered a little man, with red running-drawers, a tiny boy-like creature. He reeled as he entered and faced the roar of the applause. Then he feebly turned to the left and wearily trotted round the track. Friends and encouragers were pressing round him. Suddenly the whole group stopped. There were wild gesticulations. Men stooped and rose again. Good heavens, he has fainted: is it possible that even at this last moment the prize may slip through his fingers?… Then again he collapsed, kind hands saving him from a heavy fall. He was within a few yards of my seat. Amid stooping figures and grasping hands I caught a glimpse of the haggard, yellow face, the glazed, expressionless eyes, the lank black hair streaked across the brow.

The **1948 Olympics,** held just three years after the end of World War II, were known as "the austerity games". Olympic Games had been scheduled for 1940 and 1944, but both were cancelled; Tokyo had been meant to host the 1940 Olympics. In 1948, huge swathes of London were still in ruins from the Blitz, Britain was still experiencing rationing, and the world at large was still reeling from the war. The opening and closing ceremonies, as well as most of the events, were held at Wembley Stadium.

- The games took place from 29 July to 14 August.
- Wembley Stadium's famous greyhound track was turned into an athletics ground.
- British athletes were granted extra rations to help them cope with the physical demands of their sports.
- Male athletes were given accommodation in RAF bases on the outskirts of London; female athletes were housed in student accommodation at London colleges.
- Competitors had to take their own towels to their accommodation.
- The French Olympians brought not only their own food, but also wine.
- Germany and Japan were banned from taking part. The Soviet Union did not participate either.
- British schoolchildren were given free tickets to events.
- The cost of a ticket to stand and watch an athletics event was 3s 6d.
- The 1948 Olympics were granted a low budget of £750,000; they came in under budget at £732,268.
- This was the first Olympic Games to be shown on British TV.
- 4,000 athletes from 59 countries took part in the 1948 Olympics.

The decision to award the **2012 Olympics** to London was announced on 6 July 2005 – a day before London was horrified by the 7/7 bombings. This helped to ally the spirit of the Olympics with the spirit of London. A new Olympic Village was built in Stratford, east London. Events were also held in other areas, including Greenwich, St James's Park, Wimbledon, Wembley, Lord's Cricket Ground and Earls Court as well as venues outside London. Records were made – and broken – on and off the tracks.

- For the first time, the Paralympics were held up to equal status with the Olympics.
- It was a record year for female athletes, who made up 44 percent of competitors; women from Saudi Arabia, Brunei and Qatar took part in the games for the very first time.

- 90 percent of the British population watched the BBC's TV coverage, and in the US it was reported to be the most watched television event in history.
- London 2012 was the first Olympic Games to feature 3D broadcasting.
- 10,768 athletes from 216 countries took part.

> *I was born in Leytonstone in Waltham Forest, one of the host boroughs for the London Olympics, and I played football on Hackney Marshes as a kid, so I'm very keen to support the 2012 bid.*
>
> **David Beckham, interview in *The Telegraph*, 2004**

THE BOAT RACE

The first Oxford and Cambridge Boat Race took place on the Thames at Henley in June of 1829 – it did not involve teams of rowers but just two men, school friends, one of whom was studying in Oxford and the other at Cambridge. It became a regular event, and was relocated to London in 1836, initially at Westminster. It became an annual event in 1856. The route changed several times during the race's early history, but is now fixed between the start at Putney Bridge and the finish at Mortlake.

- The course is 6.78 km (4 miles 374 yds) long.
- The north bank of the river is known as the Middlesex side, the south bank the Surrey side.
- The Oxford crew have dark blue jerseys and oars, the Cambridge crew light blue.
- In 1859 the race ended when the Cambridge boat sank.
- Sliding seats were introduced in 1873.
- In 1877, the judges recorded the result as a draw.
- In 1938, the Boat Race was shown on BBC television for the first time.
- The first woman to participate was Oxford cox Sue Brown in 1981; her team won.
- The first Women's Boat Race took place in 1927 – but not in London. The first women's race to be rowed on the London course, and on the same day as the men's race, was on 11 April 2015.

WIMBLEDON

In 1869, The All England Croquet Club opened on Worple Road in Wimbledon. Within a couple of years it had also built facilities for the new craze of "lawn tennis". On 14 April 1877, the club changed its name to The All England Croquet and Lawn Tennis Club; in 1899 it became The All England Lawn Tennis and Croquet Club. The first Wimbledon tennis tournament took place in 1877; it is the oldest tennis tournament in the world.

- Wimbledon is the only one of the four Grand Slams still played on grass.
- The first tournament was a singles competition for men only; the first champion was Spencer Gore.
- The first Wimbledon final was postponed due to rain.
- The first men's doubles match was played in 1884, as was the first women's match.
- In 1908, Wimbledon first hosted the Olympic tennis tournament.
- There have been Wimbledon tournaments every year since 1877, except during the two world wars, 1915–18 and 1940– 45.
- In 1937, Wimbledon was televised for the first time.
- In 1940, Centre Court was bombed during the Blitz.
- In 1922, the club moved to its current location on Church Road.
- In 1967, the tournament was first broadcast on TV in colour.
- In 1968, winners started to receive prizes of money, as well as a trophy. This trophy is a replica; the original is kept by the club.
- In 1977, the Wimbledon Lawn Tennis Museum was opened.
- In 2007, male and female winners were finally awarded the same amount of prize money; until then the men had received more.
- In 2009, a retractable roof was unveiled over Centre Court.

NOTTING HILL RACECOURSE

In the nineteenth century, a large part of what is now Notting Hill was a racecourse known as the Kensington Hippodrome. It opened on 3 June 1837 – but closed down in 1842. The ground was too wet and soft to make a good racetrack, and the area was earmarked for housing instead.

SPORTS MUSEUMS

- Arsenal Football Club Museum (at the club's stadium)
- Chelsea Football Club Museum (at the club's stadium)
- Lawn Tennis Association Museum (at Wimbledon)
- MCC (Marylebone Cricket Club) Museum (at Lord's Cricket Ground)
- World Rugby Museum (at Twickenham)

IMPORTANT LONDON SPORTING VENUES

All England Lawn Tennis and Croquet Club
Crystal Palace National Sports Centre
Emirates Stadium
The Hive Stadium
Lee Valley Velo Park
Linford Christie Stadium
Loftus Road
Lord's Cricket Ground
Mile End Stadium
O2 Arena
The Oval Cricket Ground
The Queen's Club
Queen Elizabeth Olympic Park
Selhurst Park
Stamford Bridge Stadium
Twickenham Stadium
Wembley Stadium and Arena
White Hart Lane

LONDON FACTS

Lord's Cricket Ground is the only international cricket ground which is exempt from the International Cricket Council's ban on spectators bringing alcohol into cricket grounds.

DOG RACING

At the height of the popularity of greyhound (and whippet) racing, there were 25 dog-racing tracks in London. Some were shortlived, but others survived for decades.

- Battersea greyhound track on Lombard Road opened in 1930 and closed during World War II.
- The Crooked Billet greyhound track opened in the late 1920s and later became known as Walthamstow Stadium. It closed in 2008, to much heartfelt protest.
- Harlington Corner in west London (near Heathrow) opened in the 1930s and survived until the 1960s.
- Southall Stadium on Havelock Road was one of London's most popular venues from the 1930s until 1976.
- Temple Mills in Stratford opened in 1935 and survived until 1945; it was also used for boxing matches.
- Wimbledon Stadium opened in 1928 and is now the only greyhound track left in London. It hosts the annual English Greyhound Derby.

LONDON FACTS

An enduring myth about Westminster is that the "CC" logo on the borough's lamp posts are after Coco Chanel, who allegedly had an affair with the Duke of Westminster in the 1920s. The "CC" actually means City Council.

18

GHOSTS AND MYTHS

- The ghost of Anne Boleyn is said to haunt both the Tower of London and Hampton Court Palace.
- Arthur Bourchier, one-time manager of the Garrick Theatre, is rumoured to haunt the theatre. He lived in a flat inside it and is said to give actors a pat on the shoulder for good luck while they're waiting to go onstage.
- Ballet dancer Anna Pavlova is said to haunt the Palace Theatre, occasionally appearing onstage but looking as though she is standing beneath it. In her time, the stage was a couple of feet lower than today.
- The Prospect of Whitby in Wapping is alleged to be haunted by the ghost of a highwaywoman known as Moll Cutpurse.
- Room 333 of the Langham Hotel has a resident ghost: a German prince who committed suicide by throwing himself from the balcony.
- The White Woman of Berners Street, a Soho character, was one of Charles Dickens's inspirations for Miss Havisham in *Great Expectations*. He mentioned her in his magazine *Household Words* on 1 January 1853:

> *She is dressed entirely in white, with a ghastly white plaiting round her head and face, inside her white bonnet. She even carries (we hope) a white umbrella. With white boots, we know she picks her way through the winter dirt. She is a conceited old creature, cold and formal in manner, and evidently went simpering mad on personal grounds alone – no doubt because a wealthy Quaker wouldn't marry her. This is her bridal dress. She is always walking up here, on her way to church to marry the false Quaker. We observe in her mincing step and fishy eye that she intends to lead him a sharp life.*

19

LITERARY LONDON

SHERLOCK HOLMES AND BAKER STREET

- When Arthur Conan Doyle wrote his Sherlock Holmes stories, the house numbers on Baker Street did not reach as high as 221B, so he was able to give his fictional detective a fictional address.
- In the 1930s, the numbers were changed and 221B became part of the building owned by the Abbey National Building Society. So many letters were sent to Sherlock Holmes at this address that the building society eventually made answering his correspondence part of a specific job.
- The Sherlock Holmes Museum is at number 239 Baker Street.
- When the Abbey National left its building in 2002, the Royal Mail agreed that all post sent to Sherlock Holmes at 221B Baker Street would be re-routed to the museum at 239.
- In 1893, Sherlock Holmes was killed off by his inventor – but after 10 years of pleas from fans, Arthur Conan Doyle wrote another story, in which Holmes's death turned out to have been an elaborate plot to help him confuse and escape from his arch-enemy, Professor Moriarty.

THE CREATOR OF SHERLOCK HOLMES

Arthur Conan Doyle was born in Scotland on 22 May 1859. He was sent to boarding school in England at Stonyhurst College, where he was bullied viciously. He then studied medicine in Edinburgh and Vienna, before moving to London in 1891 – the same year that the first of his Sherlock Holmes stories was published in *The Strand Magazine*. He married twice, meeting his first wife, Louise Hawkins, when her brother Jack was one of his patients. They had a daughter and a son before

Louise died of tuberculosis in 1906. With his second wife, Jean Leckie, he had two sons and a daughter. He led a full life:

- As a doctor, he served with the British military in the 1900 Boer War.
- He set up a medical practice (in ophthalmology) at 2 Upper Wimpole Street, but claimed in his memoirs that no patients ever consulted him.
- He played cricket regularly with J.M. Barrie.
- In 1901, he was the judge of Britain's first major bodybuilding competition, held in Kensington.
- In 1902, he received a knighthood for his writing – not for Sherlock Holmes but for a non-fiction work about the Boer Wars.
- In 1911, he and Jean – both novice drivers – took part in the Prince Henry Tour, a competition between British and German motorcars.
- He ran for Parliament twice, unsuccessfully.
- He was friends with the escapologist Harry Houdini.
- He believed in fairies and was very excited in 1917 by a series of photographs, now known as the Cottingley Fairy photographs, which apparently showed a little girl surrounded by them.
- He was fascinated by mediums and spiritualism. After his death a huge seance was held at the Royal Albert Hall, but his spirit failed to appear.
- He was a member of the Crimes Club (founded in 1904) at which members debated real-life cases. Conan Doyle challenged and helped to change the results of two murder cases, securing the release of two prisoners, George Edalji and Oscar Slater.

LONDON IN LITERATURE

London has inspired novelists for centuries. Below is a selection of the thousands of authors and books in which it plays a prominent role:

Daniel Defoe, *Moll Flanders* (1722)
Henry Fielding, *Tom Jones* (1749)
William Makepeace Thackeray, *Vanity Fair* (1847)
Charles Dickens, *A Tale of Two Cities* (1859)
Jules Verne, *Around the World in 80 Days* (1872)
Robert Louis Stevenson, *Dr Jekyll and Mr Hyde* (1886)
Henry James, *A London Life* (1888)
George Gissing, *New Grub Street* (1891)

Oscar Wilde, *The Picture of Dorian Gray* (1891)
Somerset Maugham, *Liza of Lambeth* (1897)
E. Nesbit, *The Phoenix and the Carpet* (1904)
J.M. Barrie, *Peter Pan in Kensington Gardens* (1906)
Joseph Conrad, *The Secret Agent* (1907)
G.K. Chesterton, *The Man Who Was Thursday* (1908)
Marie Belloc Lowndes, *The Lodger* (1913)
T.S. Eliot, *The Waste Land* (1922)
Virginia Woolf, *Mrs Dalloway* (1925)
Evelyn Waugh, *Vile Bodies* (1930)
George Orwell, *Keep the Aspidistra Flying* (1936)
Noel Streatfeild, *Ballet Shoes* (1936)
Elizabeth Bowen, *The Heat of the Day* (1949)
C.P. Snow, *Homecomings* (1956)
Colin McCabe, *Absolute Beginners* (1959)
Iris Murdoch, *A Severed Head* (1961)
Agatha Christie, *At Bertram's Hotel* (1965)
A.N. Wilson, *The Sweets of Pimlico* (1977)
Iain Banks, *Walking on Glass* (1985)
Hanif Kureishi, *My Beautiful Laundrette* (1986)
Martin Amis, *London Fields* (1989)
Nick Hornby, *Fever Pitch* (1992)
Peter Ackroyd, *Hawksmoor* (1993)
Julian Barnes, *Metroland* (1997)
Helen Fielding, *Bridget Jones's Diary* (1997)
Neil Gaiman, *Neverwhere* (1997)
Zadie Smith, *White Teeth* (2001)
Keith Waterhouse, *Soho* (2001)
Monica Ali, *Brick Lane* (2003)
Zoe Heller, *Notes on a Scandal* (2003)
Sukhdhev Sandhu, *Night Haunts* (2006)
Xiaolu Guo, *A Concise Chinese-English Dictionary* (2007)
Sebastian Faulks, *A Week in December* (2006)
Audrey Niffenegger, *Her Fearful Symmetry* (2009)
John Lanchester, *Capital* (2012)
Robert Galbraith (J.K. Rowling), *Cuckoo's Calling* (2013)
Sarah Waters, *The Paying Guests* (2014)

LONDON FACTS

The first daily newspaper in Britain was the *London Gazette*. It was published for the first time on 7 November 1665.

LONDON SCI-FI

On 5 March 1891, the Royal Albert Hall hosted what is now considered the world's first science-fiction convention. It was inspired by an 1871 novel by Edward Bulwer-Lytton, originally entitled *The Coming Race*; in the early 1890s, two decades after the author's death, it was reprinted as *Vril, the Power of the Coming Race*. For the convention, the Royal Albert Hall was decorated to resemble the fictional city of Vril-ya.

QUOTATIONS ABOUT LONDON

This town … despite its lack of status was teeming with merchants and was a famous centre of commerce.

Tacitus, AD *c*.60–61

In the year of our Lord 604 … Mellitus was appointed to preach in the province of the East Saxons…. Its capital is the city of London, which stands on the banks of the Thames, and is a trading centre for many nations who visit it by land and sea.

The Venerable Bede, AD 604

Merchants bring in wares by Ships from every Nation under heaven. The Arabian sends his Gold, the Sabean his Frankincense and Spices, the Scythian Arms, Oil of Palms from the plentiful Wood: Babylon her fat Soil, and Nilus his precious Stones: the Seres send purple Garments: they and Norway and Russia Trouts, Furs and Sables: and the French their Wines.

William Fitz Stephen (d.1191)

I will fetch thee a leap
From the top of Paul's steeple to the standard in Cheap
And lead thee a dance through the streets without fail
Like a needle of Spain, with a thread at my tail.
We will survey the suburbs, and make forth our sallies
Down Petticoat Lane, and up the Smock-alleys,
To Shoreditch, Whitechapel, and so to St Kather'n's.

Ben Jonson, *The Devil Is an Ass*, 1616

You are now
In London, that great sea, whose ebb and flow
At once is deaf and loud, and on the shore
Vomits its wrecks, and still howls on for more.
Yet in its depth what treasures!

Percy Bysshe Shelley, "Letter to Maria Gisborne", 1820

What greatness had not floated on the ebb of that river into
the mystery of an unknown Earth! ... The dreams of men,
the seed of commonwealths, the germs of empire.

Joseph Conrad, *Heart of Darkness*, 1899

That's the way to get on in the world – by grabbing your
opportunities. Why, what's Big Ben but a wristwatch that
saw its chance and made good.

P.G. Wodehouse, *The Small Bachelor*, 1927

Implacable November weather. As much mud in the streets,
as if the waters had but newly retired from the face of the
earth, and it would not be wonderful to meet a Megalosaurus,
forty feet long or so, waddling like an elephantine lizard up
Holborn Hill.

Charles Dickens, *Bleak House*, 1853

Sir, when a man is tired of London, he is tired of life; for there
is in London all that life can afford.

James Boswell, *The Life of Samuel Johnson*, 1791

"In my youth, and through the prime of manhood, I never entered London without feelings of hope and pleasure. It was to me the grand theatre of intellectual activity, the field for every species of enterprise and exertion, the metropolis of the world, of business, thought, and action. There, I was sure to find friends and companions, to hear the voice of encouragement and praise. There, society of the most refined sort offered daily its banquets to the mind, and new objects of interest and ambition were constantly exciting attention either in politics, literature, or science."

These feelings, so well described by a man of genius, have probably been felt more or less by most young men who have within them any consciousness of talent, or any of that enthusiasm, that eager desire to have or to give sympathy, which, especially in youth, characterises noble natures. But after even one or two seasons in a great metropolis these feelings often change long before they are altered by age.

Maria Edgeworth, *Helen*, 1857

A mighty mass of brick, and smoke, and shipping,
Dirty and dusky, but as wide as eye
Could reach, with here and there a sail just skipping
In sight, then lost amidst the forestry
Of masts; a wilderness of steeples peeping
On tiptoe through their sea-coal canopy;
A huge, dun cupola, like a foolscap crown
On a fool's head, – and there is London Town!

Lord Byron, *"Don Juan"*, 1819

There are two places in the world where men can most effectively disappear – the city of London and the South Seas.

Herman Melville, "The South Seas", 1858–59

London is far more difficult to see properly than any other place. London is a riddle. Paris is an explanation.

G.K. Chesterton, "An Essay of Two Cities", 1874–1936

I had neither kith nor kin in England, and was therefore as free as air – or as free as an income of eleven shillings and sixpence a day will permit a man to be. Under such circumstances, I naturally gravitated to London, that great cesspool into which all the loungers and idlers of the Empire are irresistibly drained.

Sir Arthur Conan Doyle, *A Study in Scarlet*, 1887

The City seems so much more in earnest: its business, its rush, its roar, are such serious things, sights and sounds. The City is getting its living – the West-End but enjoying its pleasure.

Charlotte Bronte, *Vilette*, 1853

London is a modern Babylon.

Benjamin Disraeli, *Tancred*, 1847

At the corner of a long, straight, brick-built street in the far East End of London – one of those lifeless streets, made of two drab walls upon which the level lines, formed by the precisely even window-sills and doorsteps, stretch in weary perspective from end to end, suggesting petrified diagrams proving dead problems – stands a house that ever draws me to it; so that often, when least conscious of my footsteps, I awake to find myself hurrying through noisy, crowded thoroughfares, where flaring naphtha lamps illumine fierce, patient, leaden-coloured faces; through dim-lit, empty streets, where monstrous shadows come and go upon the close-drawn blinds; through narrow, noisome streets, where the gutters swarm with children, and each ever-open doorway vomits riot; past reeking corners, and across waste places, till at last I reach the dreary goal of my memory-driven desire, and, coming to a halt beside the broken railings, find rest.

Jerome K. Jerome, *Paul Kelver*, 1902

20

SHOPPING

A word or two respecting the daily economy of London shops. It is curious to mark the symptoms of the waking of huge London from its nightly sleep. Stage-coach travellers, unless where driven to a new system by railroads, have often means of observing this waking when entering or leaving London at a very early hour. There is an hour – after the fashionables have left their balls and parties, the rakes have reached their houses, and the houseless wanderers have found somewhere to lay their heads, but before the sober tradesmen begin the day's labour – when London is particularly still and silent ... the early breakfast-stalls, the early milkmen, and a few others, whose employment takes them into the street at an early hour. Very few shops indeed, even in the height of summer, are opened before six o'clock; but at that hour the apprentices and shopmen may be seen taking down the shutters from the windows.... The splendour of modern shops has in some cases reached to the shutters themselves, which are highly polished, and not unfrequently figured and decorated with gold.... When the shutters, whatever be their kind, are taken down, we soon see busy indications of cleansing operations going on: how sedulously the glass is wiped, the floor swept, the counters dusted, let the busy apprentice tell. Then comes the shopman or the master, who lays out in the window the goods intended to be displayed that day ... in many the shop-window is cleared every evening, again to be filled the next morning.

Charles Knight, *Knight's London*, 1842

FORTNUM & MASON

In 1707, a royal footman named William Fortnum began a fruitful business partnership with his landlord, a market trader called Hugh Mason. Fortnum was in the employment of Queen Anne and began to make extra money by collecting the candles that the Royal Family discarded after just one evening's use – they insisted on new candles every day. By selling the candles, Fortnum began to amass savings. Together Fortnum and Mason set up a shop in Piccadilly. From the start, the Royal Family gave it their patronage and its reputation grew. It has remained a London institution ever since, famous for luxury goods and picnic hampers.

WHITELEYS

In the 1840s, William Whiteley left his native Yorkshire for the bright lights of London. His dream was to create a shopping emporium that would persuade people not only to visit his stores but to linger and turn shopping into a daytrip. His first shop, in Westbourne Grove, became the very first department store, but burnt down in 1887. By this time Whiteley was a major name in London, famous for his vision and the way he treated his 6,000 staff, many of whom lived in staff accommodation; he was also famous in the surrounding countryside, where he owned farms and factories to provide food for his staff and customers. His vision then turned to a newer, more elegant empire – the current Whiteleys in Bayswater, which dates back to 1911. Unfortunately, William Whiteley died four years before the new building was finished, and in very dramatic circumstances: he was murdered by a man who claimed to be his illegitimate son. His killer, Horace Rayner, was hanged after a one-day trial. The jury were unanimous and took just nine minutes to deliver their verdict.

THE EXETER CHANGE

This eighteenth-century shopping arcade on The Strand was famous for housing a menagerie of exotic animals that customers could visit.

ST JAMES'S STREET AND SURROUNDINGS

Including Jermyn Street, the area has been famous for its shops since the seventeenth century. Some of London's most famous names can be found within a short walk of St James's Palace:

- Berry Bros & Rudd
- Church's
- Czech & Speake
- Harvie & Hudson
- James J. Fox
- John Lobb
- Lock & Co Hatters
- Geo F. Trumper
- Paxton & Whitfield
- Trufitt & Hill
- Turnbull & Asser

HARRODS

- Harrods was founded in 1834 by Charles Henry Harrod, a 25-year-old tea merchant, in Stepney.
- The original shop was a one-room grocery store. Today Harrods stands on over 2 ha (5 acres) of land and has 330 departments.
- In 1849, the shop moved to Knightsbridge.
- The current shop building was built in the early 1900s by architect Richard Burbidge, and opened in 1905.
- The store's motto is *omnia omnibus ubique*: "everything for everybody everywhere".
- For decades Harrods promised its customers that it could provide anything they wanted, from an elephant to an aeroplane.
- The famous lighted façade of Harrods uses around 12,000 lightbulbs; around 300 have to be changed every day.
- In 1917, Harrods opened an in-store zoo.
- Noel Coward bought an alligator at Harrods and in 1967, the Hollywood actor Ronald Reagan was given a baby elephant as a gift, which had been bought at Harrods.

- The original Winnie-the-Pooh, which inspired A.A. Milne to write his famous books, was a teddy bear bought at Harrods as a present for his son Christopher Robin.
- In 2010, Harrods owners Mohammed and Ali Al-Fayed sold it to Qatar Holdings for an alleged £1.5 billion.

LIBERTY

On 15 May 1875, an exciting new shop opened in London and quickly became the store of choice for those in Aesthetic and Bohemian art circles – and those who wanted to be. Arthur Lasenby Liberty's ambition was to change the way the general public looked at fashion and interior design. His first shop, at 218a Regent Street, was just half a shop, but within a decade he had made enough money to pay off his loan and move to much larger premises, 142–144 Regent Street. Within two years, the South Kensington Museum (the future V&A) had bought antique textiles from Liberty, encouraging other style-setters to do the same, and gradually the shop became a London icon. Arthur Liberty died in 1917, but his shop thrived. Through the end of the Aesthetic nineteenth century and into the eras of Art Nouveau and the Bright Young Things, Liberty was at the forefront of fashion. The current building, with its unforgettable "half-timbered" Mock Tudor façade on Great Marlborough Street, was created in 1924. It was designed by father-and-son architects Edwin T. Hall and Edwin S. Hall, and used the timbers of two ships, HMS *Impregnable* and HMS *Hindustan*.

> *Liberty is the chosen resort of the artistic shopper.*
> *Oscar Wilde*

OTHER FAMOUS LONDON SHOPS

- Army & Navy Store (no longer in existence)
- Barkers (no longer in existence)
- Biba (no longer in existence)
- Debenham & Freebody (now Debenhams)

- F.W. Woolworth & Co (no longer in existence)
- Fortnum & Mason
- Harrods
- Harvey Nichols
- Hyper Hyper (no longer in existence)
- I Was Lord Kitchener's Valet (no longer in existence)
- John Lewis
- Liberty
- Lord John (no longer in existence)
- Marks & Spencer
- Peter Jones
- Selfridges
- Sex (no longer in existence)

LONDON SHOP FACTS

- There has been a tobacco shop on the site of James J. Fox since 1787; the first was opened by Robert Lewis, whose company was eventually bought by James J. Fox. The shop is one of the few places in London that is exempt from the smoking ban. At the back is a small cigar museum, with memorabilia from the shop's most famous customers, including King Edward VII, Oscar Wilde and Sir Winston Churchill.
- Lock & Co is one of the world's oldest milliners. It was established in 1676 and has created some of history's most famous hats, including Lord Nelson's bicorn hat (a replica of which can now be seen at the top of Nelson's Column).
- Berry Bros & Rudd is the oldest wine merchant in the country, and has been supplying the Royal Family with wines and spirits since the reign of George III.

NOTABLE LONDON BOOKSHOPS

FOYLES

- Founded in 1903 as a mail-order business by brothers William and Gilbert Foyle.
- They had failed their civil service exams so sold off their textbooks.
- In 1904, they moved to the West End, taking on a shop in Cecil Court.

- In 1906, Foyles moved to Charing Cross Road, specializing in educational books.
- After the First World War, the brothers bought a site further up Charing Cross Road and built a new, much larger bookshop.
- By the 1940s, there were four other branches of Foyles, in Ireland and South Africa.
- William retired in 1945, and his daughter Christina took over control of the shop.
- After her death in 1999, the business passed to her nephew, Christopher.
- He opened several new branches, and in 2014 the shop moved to a bigger flagship store, also on Charing Cross Road.

HATCHARD'S

- In 1797, John Hatchard left his job working for bookseller Thomas Payne.
- He leased a small premises at 173 Piccadilly and set up his own bookselling business.
- By the summer of 1801, Hatchard's was doing so well that he moved to 189&190 Piccadilly; the buildings have since been renumbered, but the shop remains in the same premises.
- Following John's death in 1849, the business remained in the family until the 1880s.
- It continued as an independent bookshop for another century, until bought by Waterstones in the 1990s.

WATERSTONES PICCADILLY

- When the small bookselling chain Waterstones bought a former department store on Piccadilly in 1999, it made literary history.
- The company's new flagship store was the biggest bookshop in Europe, with six floors.
- The Art Deco building was originally a famous department store, Simpson. As it is a listed building, permitting very few architectural changes, the name of the previous occupier is still visible.

21

BED AND BOARD

HOTELS

- The Savoy Hotel opened in 1889, to cater to American tourists. It was the first hotel in London to give all its bedrooms en-suite bathrooms.
- In the nineteenth century, an inventor from Birmingham, John Webb, came up with a new design of gas lamp – powered by methane from sewage. Although there were several, only one remains in London. It is in Carting Lane, alongside the Savoy Hotel and Theatre. Today it is dual-powered by the main gas supply as well as methane sewage.
- Brown's Hotel on Albermarle Street was opened by Lord Byron's former valet James Brown. Rudyard Kipling wrote part of *The Jungle Book* at Brown's and Agatha Christie was allegedly inspired by the venue to write *At Bertram's Hotel*.
- Claude Monet stayed at the Savoy in 1900 and 1901, so he could paint the views Turner had painted from the bank of the Thames before the hotel was built. Monet insisted on having the same suite both years, so his view would be identical. He found the grey London smog a bonus for painting, but hated the way it made him feel depressed and blocked out sunshine.
- The Langham Hotel was the first London hotel to install electricity.
- The Savoy was the first to have hot and cold running water in every bedroom and 24-hour service.
- In 1944, General Eisenhower planned the Normandy Invasion from the Dorchester Hotel, which had been turned into his headquarters.
- In 2010, London hosted the world's smallest pop-up hotel: a converted airstream caravan at Alexandra Palace.

EATING AND DRINKING

- Rowley's Restaurant on Jermyn Street is located where entrepreneur Thomas Wall once lived. His name lives on in Wall's Ice Cream – even though he began as a seller of meat products. The company Thomas Wall and Son started selling ice creams in 1922, from mobile stalls on tricycles.
- The oldest restaurant in London is Rules on Maiden Lane. Although the records are missing, it is believed that a Thomas Rule began selling oysters and other snacks here in the late 1790s. The restaurant stayed in the Rule family for over a century, then shortly before World War I, it passed to Tom Bell, a British restaurateur living in Paris. It remained in his family until 1984, when it was bought by John Mayhew.
- The Wolseley restaurant on Piccadilly used to be a famous 1920s car showroom. The lavish building, designed for Wolseley Car Company by architect William Curtis Green, proved too expensive to sustain. Within five years the company was bankrupt and in 1926 the building was bought by Barclays Bank. It opened as a restaurant in 2003.
- Simpson's-in-the-Strand opened in 1928 as a coffee house and chess club. Meals were served beside chess players, rather than in front of them.

LONDON FACTS

The oldest surviving Indian restaurant in England is Veeraswamy, on Regent Street, which opened in 1926.

FAMOUS LONDONERS

The artist **James Mallord William Turner** was born in Maiden Lane, Covent Garden in 1775, the son of a barber and wigmaker. He showed early talent for drawing, and his father offered his son's pictures for sale in his shop. In 1789, aged 14, he was admitted to the Royal Academy, the school's youngest pupil to date. He exhibited there in 1790, and for the next 60 years. A proud Cockney all his life, Turner was buried in 1851 in the crypt of St Paul's Cathedral alongside artists such as Van Dyck and Reynolds.

22

ANIMALS

BEAR BAITING AND BULL BAITING

In order to gratify his Highness, and at his desire, two bears and a bull were baited…. Four dogs at once were set on the bull; they, however, could not gain any advantage over him, for he so artfully contrived to ward off their attacks that they could not well get at him; on the contrary, the bull served them very scurvily by striking and butting at them.

Letter written by Frederick, Duke of Württemberg,
visiting London, 1 September 1592

For centuries, these were popular London pastimes. Special arenas were built where hungry dogs were set upon a tethered bull or bear. During the Tudor era there was a bullring and "bear garden" in Southwark. In 1583, its wooden scaffolding collapsed, killing eight people.

Gradually the sport became more competitive and dogs were specially bred; this is where the "British bulldog" breed originates. Most dogs were killed during the baiting fights, but survivors became celebrities and large amounts of money were gambled on favoured bulldogs and mastiffs. Samuel Pepys described bull-baiting in his diary on 14 August 1666 as "a very rude and nasty pleasure".

Although the practice had largely disappeared by the end of the eighteenth century, it was not outlawed, as a letter to the *Morning Post* in November 1828 attests: "Sir, The disgraceful extent to which bull-baiting, which had of late been in a great degree abolished, has now been resumed, is shewn in the following letter" [to the newly formed Society for the Prevention of Cruelty to Animals]. In 1835, the Cruelty to Animals Act was passed in Parliament, making bull and bear baiting, as well as cockfighting, illegal.

LONDON FACTS

During the late eighteenth century, in the reign of William and Mary, a French visitor wrote of seeing a bull garlanded with ribbons and flowers being paraded through the streets of London prior to being taken to the bullring and baited to death.

COCKFIGHTING

Popular for centuries, in the eighteenth century cockfighting became particularly fashionable – and lucrative for bookmakers. In 1759, William Hogarth published his engraving *The Cockpit* which shows two birds fighting in a small table-top arena surrounded by a depraved caricatured mob; many of the spectators were recognizable to contemporary viewers. Cockfighting took place all over London and is commemorated in a number of place names, including Cockpit Steps in SW1, the Cock Tavern on Fleet Street and the Cock Pit pub on St Andrew's Hill. Cockpit Steps, close to Birdcage Walk, shows the sinister side of the royal aviary: the eighteenth-century Royal Cockpit was intended to give the upper classes their own venue, where the clientele was richer and betting stakes higher.

HUNTING

- Many of London's parks were once royal hunting grounds.
- In the Tudor period, the area around modern Oxford Street and Soho was still fields and woodland, popular for hunting with horses and dogs.
- On Marylebone High Street is a plaque to the thirteenth-century Tyburn Manor House, a hunting lodge used by Henry VIII and Elizabeth I.
- The area now Richmond Park had been used for hunting by generations of kings, but it was Charles I who turned it into a deer park, in 1637. He wanted to hunt outside plague-ridden London.

TRAFALGAR SQUARE

Long before it was laid out as a landscaped square, the area around what is now Trafalgar Square was part of the Royal Mews for Whitehall Palace. The word "mews" derives from the French *muer* meaning to moult, indicative of the hunting birds originally housed here while moulting. Later mews were also used for stabling horses.

LONDON FACTS

In the past, now-desirable mews houses were the stables and coach-houses behind grand houses, where only animals and the poorest servants slept. In *The Chimes*, one of Charles Dickens's lesser-known Christmas books, the kindly Trotty Veck offers to help a stranger, but apologizes for inviting him to a poor mews house.

THE TOWER MENAGERIE

- There are records of wild animals at the Tower of London dating back to 1210 and the reign of King John.
- James I had a passion for animal-baiting and had a private baiting den built at the Tower.
- When the Tower became a tourist attraction, visitors could pay to see the royal menagerie.
- In the 1830s, the Duke of Wellington, who was the Constable of the Tower, sent the menagerie animals to London Zoo in Regent's Park.

LONDON ZOO

- The Zoological Society of London was founded by explorer and statesman Sir Thomas Stamford Raffles in 1826.
- In 1828, the zoo was opened in Regent's Park to Fellows of the Zoological Society. Friends and family could also visit, on payment of the entrance fee and bearing a letter written by a Fellow. From 1847, the public was permitted to enter.
- Charles Darwin became a Fellow in 1837.
- When the hippopotamus Obaysch arrived, he was the first live hippo in

Europe. He became a celebrity and his photograph was sold to tourists.
- In 1881, the zoo opened the world's first "insect house".
- In the twentieth century, public opinion of zoos changed. The ZSL purchased a larger area of land outside London, at Whipsnade, to give animals more room. Controversially, it still kept many of its larger animals in cages in Regent's Park.
- In the 1960s, rules were passed forbidding visitors to feed the animals.
- Over the years, the zoo had 12 giant pandas, including the popular Chi-Chi who arrived in 1958, and Ching-Ching and Chia-Chia in 1974.

BIRDS OF ST JAMES'S PARK

King James I introduced a menagerie into what is now St James's Park. He imported camels, an elephant and even two crocodiles, and added a number of exotic birds. A gigantic aviary was built on what is now called Birdcage Walk. In 1664, the Russian Ambassador to the Court of St James presented Charles II with a pair of pelicans, the first to be seen in the park.

A PRIVATE MENAGERIE IN CHELSEA

In the early 1860s, the recently widowed Pre-Raphaelite artist Dante Gabriel Rossetti moved into 16 Cheyne Walk. He collected a menagerie of exotic animals, including peacocks, armadillos, wallabies and his much-loved wombat. Unfortunately he had little understanding of exotic animals, and most of them died.

BEARS AND BEARDS

In the eighteenth and nineteenth centuries, a popular product for use on hair and beards was "bear's grease". Barbers would put up a notice announcing when they were about to kill a bear, believed by gullible customers to be kept in a cellar under the shop. It seems that the same bear was handed from shop to shop, permanently about to meet its doom. The "bear grease" meanwhile was obtained from another, less rare and presumably less expensive animal.

OTHER TITLES IN THIS SERIES INCLUDE:

THE TUDOR TREASURY
A collection of fascinating
facts and insights about the
Tudor dynasty
Elizabeth Norton
ISBN: 9780233004334

THE AGINCOURT
COMPANION
A guide to the legendary battle
and warfare in the medieval world
Anne Curry
ISBN: 9780233004716

MAGNA CARTA
AND ALL THAT
A guide to the Magna Carta
and life in England in 1215
Rod Green
ISBN: 9780233004648

THE VICTORIAN TREASURY
A collection of fascinating
facts and insights about
the Victorian Era
Lucinda Hawksley
ISBN: 9780233004778